Contents

Edexcel A2 English Language: Introduction

Welcome to the second year of your English Language A-level course. In this year you will study the development of English into a world language with over 350 million native speakers and the sheer diversity of English that exists across the world. You will also look at the development of language in young children – how they acquire spoken language and how they develop written language.

How does A2 build on AS?

In Units 1 and 2 you developed a range of skills. You looked at issues such as style, context and pragmatics. You learned about the key constituents of language. You were introduced to a range of language theory and learned how to apply it. You learned how to analyse language and how to write for a very specific genre and a selected audience. In Units 3 and 4, you will develop these skills further. You will be introduced to further language theory and learn to study it, taking a critical and open-minded approach. You will also be encouraged to develop your own theories about language.

What will I learn?

Unit 3 Language diversity and children's language development

English changes over time and it changes across the world. You will study the origins of English – Where did the most widely spoken language in the world come from? You will also study the amazing varieties of English that exist within the United Kingdom and across the world today. You will also look at the development of language in individuals – at how children become competent language producers and receivers of both spoken and written language in a very short space of time.

Unit 4 English Language investigation and presentation

You will have the opportunity to follow your own specific interests in the wide field of English language study by carrying out your own research investigation into an aspect of language you have chosen. The world of English language is your oyster. You will carry out preparation for your research, which will include producing a short article, talk or presentation about your topic area. You will also collect and analyse data, using the skills and understanding you have developed during your study of A-level English Language, to carry out your own piece of linguistic research.

How will I be assessed?

Unit 3 is assessed by an external exam. Unit 4 is assessed by coursework.

Unit 3

Unit 3 accounts for 30% of the marks for the whole GCE course and is assessed by a 2 hour 45 minute external exam. You have to comment on texts related to the language issues you have studied.

Edexcel A2 English Language

Danuta Reah   Craig Newton   Alison Ross

STUDENT BOOK

Consultant: Jen Greatrex

Skills Coverage Map

Skill/specification coverage	UNIT 3	UNIT 4
Exploring how English has changed over time	9-29, 41-46	
Exploring different forms of English around the world	29-46	
Defining English	9-12	
Understanding Standard English	12-14, 25-29	
Exploring the origins of English	12-13	
Understanding vocabulary	14-19, 27-29, 31, 34-35, 36-37, 40-41	
Understanding grammar	15-17, 32, 34, 37, 39-40, 59-64	
Exploring regional variation (dialect)	25-27, 41	
Exploring American English	30-32	
Understanding pronunciation and phonology	31, 33-34, 38, 39, 68-69, 82-84	
Understanding spelling and orthography	32, 82-84	
Exploring African American Vernacular English	33	
Exploring Australian English	33-35	
Exploring pidgins and creoles	36-38	
Exploring Indian English	38-41	
Understanding children's spoken language	47-72, 93-97	
Understanding children's written language	73-97	
Exploring theories of learning language	47, 48-55	
Exploring theories of the nature of language	47, 56-73	
Understanding the structural approach to language	56-69	
Understanding the functional approach to language	56, 69-73	
Understanding morphology	65-66	
Understanding lexis and semantics	66	
Understanding the effect of culture and environment	27-29, 67, 74-79, 92	126-127
Understanding discourse and pragmatics	71-73, 80-81	
Understanding genre conventions	71	
Understanding signs and symbols	74-75, 82, 85	
Understanding research		100-105
Choosing a topic for research		106-108
Managing your time		109-111
Writing an article, talk or presentation		112-120
Carrying out a research investigation		121-163
Choosing a research method		123-127
Collecting data for research		127-139
Collecting spoken language data		132-136
Collecting written language data		136
Analysing research data		140-154
Drawing conclusions from research data		155-156
Writing a research report		157-163

Unit 4

Unit 4 accounts for 20% of the marks for the whole GCE course. You have to produce a short talk, article or presentation for an informed but non-expert audience as part of your investigation preparation and you have to carry out a research investigation and write it up in a report format. You will submit both pieces in a coursework folder for your assessment.

How to use this book

The **Student Book** is designed to support you with each of the A2 units by providing:

- clear explanations of what is required of you and how you will be assessed
- a wide range of texts relating to the areas the book covers, along with activities to build the skills you need in understanding the language issues involved
- guidance in approaching exam and coursework tasks to help you understand what the examiners are looking for and how you can achieve your full potential.

The Student Book is divided into Unit 3 and Unit 4. **Unit 3** supports your work for the A2 exam 'Language diversity and children's language development'. **Unit 4** supports your work for the A2 coursework component, 'English language investigation and presentation'.

The **Teaching and Assessment CD-ROM** provides additional support, including commentaries, explanations of linguistic concepts and further texts and exemplar responses. It can be used alongside this book.

Unit 3: Language diversity and children's language development

Unit 3 in the Student Book is divided into two sections, reflecting the topics the exam covers. They are:

Section A: Language diversity (pp 8–46)

In this section, you will study the way language has changed over time and the ways it varies socially, culturally, nationally and internationally. You will develop the skills of identifying, commenting on and applying the key constituents of language.

Section B: Children's language development (pp 47–97)

In this section, you will study the way that children develop the skills of written and spoken language, and study the theories and research that relate to this language area. To listen to the audio files accompanying this section, visit **www.edexcel.com/cld-mp3**

Unit 4: English Language investigation and presentation

Unit 4 in the Student Book is divided into three sections:

Section A: Approaching your coursework

This section will guide you in choosing a topic that interests you, and one that is suitable for investigation. You will also learn how to manage your time.

Section B: Task 1

In this section you will study a range of formats and develop skills in writing about language topics in a way that suits your format and audience.

Section C: Task 2

In this section you will develop the skills of data collection, data analysis, understanding the significance of your findings and drawing conclusions for them. You will also learn how to write a report.

Unit 3: Language diversity and children's language development

Unit introduction

In Unit 3 of Edexcel A2 English Language, you will:

- explore the origins and development of the English language
- learn how to analyse texts from a variety of different periods and contexts
- explore the role of English in the world today and its development as an international and second language
- investigate children's spoken and written language development from the earliest sounds and letter-like forms to the development of pragmatic, narrative and descriptive skills
- expand and apply the 'toolkit' of terminology for describing language use
- consider theories and research related to diversity and children's language acquisition
- build on the knowledge and skills gained at AS level.

The course

What you will do in the exam (2 hours 45 minutes)

In **Section A**, you will explore language diversity over time and in global contexts. There are two questions in Section A and both are data based:

- For question 1 (a), you will provide short responses identifying specific ways in which the data shows language change or ways in which social and cultural varieties differ (10 marks).
- For question 1 (b), you will examine longer pieces of data and produce a more in-depth response (40 marks).

In **Section B**, you will explore children's spoken and/or written language development. Again there are two questions, both data based:

- For question 2 (a), based on short data extracts, you will produce short responses demonstrating how the data exemplifies specific aspects of the development process (10 marks).
- For question 2 (b), you will produce a longer answer showing knowledge of the process of children's language development and relevant theories (40 marks).

What the examiners are looking for

Examiners use three Assessment objectives (AOs) to mark your answers.

Assessment objective	What this means in practice
AO1 Select and apply a range of linguistic methods to communicate relevant knowledge using appropriate terminology and coherent, accurate written expression.	You should use: • relevant concepts from linguistic study • precise and detailed linguistic terminology • a clear style of writing.
AO2 Demonstrate critical understanding of a range of concepts and issues related to the construction and analysis of meanings in spoken and written language, using knowledge of linguistic approaches.	You should apply: • relevant ideas to show how language conveys meaning • knowledge of theories and research about language use • awareness of social attitudes.
AO3 Analyse and evaluate the influence of contextual factors on the production and reception of spoken and written language, showing knowledge of the key constituents of language.	You should show: • knowledge of time and place • understanding of their influence on language use • ability to analyse language at various levels.

Section A Language diversity

Part 1 is concerned with one aspect of diversity – how English has changed over time. The main focus of this part is to explore some of the changes that the English language has undergone over time as a result of social, political, cultural and technological influences. Modern versions of texts are examined alongside older forms to help you explore how English has changed over time in response these influences.

Part 2 is concerned with the diverse forms of English used around the world. In the first sub-section you will explore the lexis, grammar, phonology and orthography of English as a first language. In subsequent sub-sections, creole forms of English will be explored. You will also cover English as a second language and its position as a world language. The final brief sub-section looks at the diversity of English within the UK.

Section B Children's language development

Part 1 examines and explores the development of a child's spoken language. Through the analysis of transcripts and other data, you will explore how children develop the key constituents of language and explore their use of language from the earliest sounds to sophisticated language use. By examining examples of language in use, you will also consider relevant theories and research that attempt to explain how and why language develops.

Part 2 explores the ways children learn to write. You will explore the process, which starts with an understanding that signs can communicate meaning and develops into an ability to express more complex ideas in the written mode. You will also learn how children interpret and understand written language, as well as relevant theories and research. You will also consider other issues, such as whether the process is linked to the development of spoken language and the effects of social and cultural factors on a child's earliest writing.

How to succeed in English Language Unit 3

- Make sure you are familiar with all the information you learned at AS, as this can be applied alongside the new information at A2.
- Acknowledge doubts and accept the existence of 'grey areas'.
- Try and read a wide range of texts from different times – they will become less strange the more you read them.
- Make yourself familiar with global diversity. Keep your linguistic head on when watching television or other media – you are exposed to English from other countries all the time.
- Observe children's speech in action. Think about how what you hear relates to your studies and develop your own ideas about the development of children's language.
- If you are able, acquire more examples of children's written language; for example, your own early written language may be available to you. Explore any resources you can gather in light of the theories and research into the development of written language.

Section A: Language diversity

Section A focuses on two aspects of diversity. The ways in which English has changed over time as a result of external forces is explored in part 1. In part 2, you will explore forms of English from other parts of the globe and examine how they differ from other forms of English.

The English language is not, and never has been, a static and stable entity existing in only one form. Like all living things, it adapts to an ever-changing environment by undergoing changes itself.

One of the most noticeable areas of change has been over time. Social, political and technological developments have all acted on the English language and have caused it to undergo significant changes. Although the speed and scope of change has slowed over the last few hundred years, the English we use today is different in some ways to that used even 50 years ago. This is especially true of spoken English, which tends to be more susceptible to change. Part 1 covers language change over time and answers some of the basic questions such as 'Where did English come from?', 'How has it changed?' and 'What have been the major influences on its modern form?'

The notion of change also includes geographical diversity. As English speakers travel, contacts with other languages and cultures have shaped and altered the English language further. Colonisation of other lands has led to people speaking different forms of English settling together and so given rise to more diverse forms of English, which have evolved independently from the form spoken in England. Part 2 therefore explores the forms of English that we encounter around the globe. Other variables, many of which you studied at AS, such as gender and social class, also influence the development of other forms that are distinct from Standard English.

With these changes in mind, it becomes increasingly difficult to think of what we can call *the English language* and instead we have to start thinking of different forms of English or Englishes.

This section covers the learning required for Section A of the Unit 3 exam. The exam has two questions, worth a total of 50 marks (50% of the whole exam):

- a short response to a piece of data (10 marks)
- a longer response to a selection of longer pieces of data (40 marks).

The texts for analysis will be drawn from a variety of different contexts. Although all the texts will have a common theme, they will exemplify aspects of diversity. This may mean that they could be older forms of English, as used either in the British Isles or anywhere else where English has seeded, or that they reflect modern global diversity and be drawn from different English-speaking communities.

Assessment objectives

AO1 marks are awarded for selecting and applying a range of linguistic methods to communicate relevant knowledge using appropriate terminology and coherent, accurate written expression. (10 marks from a total of 50)

AO2 marks are awarded for demonstrating critical understanding of a range of concepts and issues related to the construction and analysis of meanings in spoken and written language, using knowledge of linguistic approaches. (20 marks from a total of 50)

AO3 marks are awarded for analysing and evaluating the influence of contextual factors on the production and reception of spoken and written language, showing knowledge of the key constituents of language. (20 marks from a total of 50)

1 English over time

English today

Before exploring the changes that English has undergone as a result of external and internal influences over time, it is useful to look at *what* and *where* English is today. You have spent at least the last year studying the English language and for many of you it is a language you have used for your whole life. But you have probably never stopped to think about what English *is* and how to define it.

- Is it the language you or your friends use?
- Is it best illustrated by somebody in authority such as newsreaders or the Queen?
- Is it the language you see in Internet chat rooms or the messages posted on social networking sites?
- Is it the language you hear in Hollywood movies and American sitcoms?
- Is it the language you hear from rappers and musicians on MTV?

There are so many diverse forms. Which is English? Are they all English?

Each of you will have different views of what English is, as well as different experiences of its use. You are probably much more aware of what you think isn't English (but even then you have to be careful, as you will see throughout this section), but what *is* English is a much more fluid question.

Activity 1

Working in groups, try to define English. What makes a language English? Where is English found? Who speaks it?

Activity 2

1 Read the following extracts and match them up with the descriptions on page 11.

2 Now discuss the following questions:

   a Which seem to be forms of English?

   b Can you supply some evidence from relevant key constituents of language (phonology/graphology, morphology, lexis, grammar and discourse) to back up your decisions?

   c Where would each variety of language be used? Who would use it and in what context?

Text A

Aa myed me way doon te the Central Station and got a tram the trams wor runnin in them days. Off alang Scotswood Road we gans. Wey ye knaa whaat the aad trams wor like – the' swung aboot like hikeys. As we got near te Clumbor Street aa myed me way te the stairs haadin the rail wi one hand and the flooers high abuv me head wi the uthor, when suddenly she stops! Aa just cuddent help mesell; doon the stairs aa cyem cowpin me
5 kreels at the bottom and oot aa shoots ontiv the road...

Aa opened me eyes and aal aa cud see wor fyesses lyeukin doon, and for aal the shootin neebody did nowt.

Text B

Hi r u stll meetin me at mment @ 6? Hob sed u wud brng the nu dvd – ya got it? If not do not fuss. C u soon. F x

Text C: from *Cell Signalling* by John T. Hancock (1997)

Phosphorylation is also crucial in the activation of other isoforms. PLCγ is phosphorylated on some tyrosine residues, usually those at positions 771, 783 and 1254. This may be catalysed by a tyrosine kinase linked receptor, for example the EGF receptor.

Text D

Den, Fox staat fuh talk. E say to eself, a say, 'Dish yuh Crow duh ooman, enty? Ef a kin suade um fuh talk, him haffuh op'n e mout, enty? En ef e op'n e mout, enty de meat fuh drop out?'
Fox call to de Crow: 'Mawnin tittuh,' 'e say. 'Uh so glad you tief da meat fum de buckruh, cause him bin fuh trow-um-way pan de dog ... E mek me bex fuh see man do shishuh ting lukkuh dat.'

Text E

hi:
Heya, how are you doing recently? I would like to introduce you a very good company which i knew. Their company homepage is wwx.xxxxx.com. They can offer you all kinds of electronical products which you need, such as motorcycles, laptops, mobile phones, digial cameras, TV LCD, xbox, ps3, gps, MP3/4, etc. Please take
5   some time to have a look at it, there must be something you'd like to purchase.
Their website: wwx.xxxx.com
Their contact email: xxxx@.com
MSN: xxxx@xxx.xx
TEL: +xxxxxxxx
10   Hope you have a good mood in shopping from their company!
Best Regards!

Text F

Wi the recent needcessity for the Cross Pairtie Comatee on Scots ti translate an offeecial blad inti Scots, the leid finnds itsel at a turnin pynt. For a gey lang time, the'r been fowk threipin at Scots shoud be traetit as a langage in its ain richt. At the same time, the'r been fowk – whiles the same fowk – threipin at Scots is only uiss for leeterary ettles, an at English can be uised for aa the practical wark. But ye canna pit Scots forrit as a langage on the same foond as Gaelic an no can write offeecial blads in it, like ye can wi Gaelic.

Text G

B: O you want /wæn/ the /di/ computer now

O: why

B: I just /jus/ de ask /ax/ if you want /wæn/ the /di/ computer now

O: Yeah (.) I come /com/ get it now

B: OK then come / com/get it.

Text H

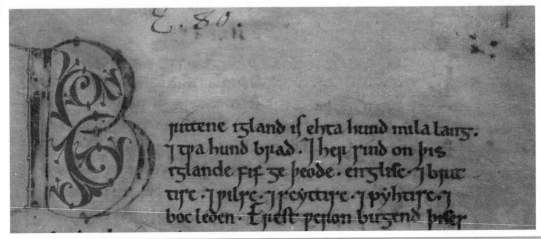

Text I

A vox gon out of þe wode go
Afingret so þat him wes wo
He nes neuere in none wise
Afingret erour half so swiþe.
5 He ne hoeld nouþer wey ne strete
For him wes loþ men to mete.
Him were leuere meten one hen
þen half an oundred wimmen.
He strok swiþe oueral
10 So þat he ofsei ane wal.
Wiþinne þe walle wes on hous.
The wox wes þider swiþe wous
For he þohute his hounger aquenche
Oþer mid mete oþer mid drunche.

Descriptions

- A very early form of English – Old English
- A text message
- An example of modern scientific writing
- An example of 'Lallans' – the Scots language, written down
- An example of 'Geordie' English as spoken in the north-east of England
- Another early form of English – Middle English (southern dialect).
- A very short extract from conversation between teenage girls living in Newcastle, who originally came from the Caribbean
- An example of 'Gullah', spoken in South Carolina and Georgia , North America, by some African Americans
- An example of a 'spam email'

Writing in the exam

Remember to link language forms to **context**, as this is something the examiner will be looking for.

Key term

- context

Writing in the exam

You will not be asked questions in the exam about these very early forms of English. Texts used in the exam will not be earlier than the start of the early modern English period, which is generally agreed to be towards the end of the 15th century.

You may have been surprised that some of the forms above are classed as English because they may well have differed from your expectations of what English is. This may be especially true of forms like Gullah. How can it be English if you don't understand it? There are so many diverse forms of English today that even people who identify as English speakers may not even understand each other.

'English' has been around for some 1500 years and over that time it has shown itself to be highly variable and continually changing. These changes can be linked to contacts with other languages via invasion, trade, colonialism and immigration, some can be linked to social and cultural changes within British society, some to developments in science and technology. Other changes can be linked to the spread of English geographically. English has spread throughout the UK, then across the globe. Millions of users put it to different uses in a many different places and this has caused the language to change.

'English' does not just mean those obvious varieties such as standard British English or even global forms such American English. Each area that uses English has its own forms that are thought of 'standard' for that area, and they are all English.

How do we define English?

Because of the diverse number of forms, defining just what English is quite difficult and several views can be taken.

There is the popular but narrow view that defines English only in terms of educated use – the standard form. Books on grammar and style have a tendency towards this viewpoint. Most books on grammar, or those that promote the idea that there is a correct and an incorrect form of English, base the grammar of the language on the written form. As you will have observed during your study at AS-level, spoken language is the more widely used form and its grammar is very different from the grammar of written language. This view of language excludes the vast majority of daily language and doesn't sufficiently cover the texts you have already examined.

But there is another way of approaching language – one that is not so restrictive and, ultimately, so unrealistic. If you ask a Californian, a Texan, a Jamaican, somebody from Yorkshire or an Australian what language they speak, the answer will be 'English'. Yet these forms may not always be fully mutually understood – an issue you may have encountered.

The origins of English

The origins of English lie in the 5th century with the arrival in the British Isles of the Germanic tribes from Continental Europe. Later, in the 8th and 9th centuries, Viking invaders from the Scandinavian countries colonised the eastern part of England. In the 11th century came the Norman invasion, which brought the French language to the existing mix of Germanic, Latin and Celtic languages.

To what extent are these very early forms of English still found in the modern language used today?

Activity 3

1 Using the dictionary, look at the origins of the following words:

the	knee	I	you	and	father
bread	for	of	shirt	in	daughter
sister	to	hat	egg	heart	on

2 Divide them into grammatical words (words that form part of the structure of the language, like auxiliary verbs, prepositions, pronouns, conjunctions; these words are often hard to define, other than by describing their function) and 'lexical' words that have a clear dictionary meaning or content.

3 Group the lexical words into semantic fields.

   a Which fields can you identify?

   b Why have these groups of words remained in the language from such an early period? Identify other words from these semantic fields that are still in current use and look up their origins. Are these from the same or from a later period?

   c Are there other semantic fields where you might expect to find words from very early periods?

English as a national language

Through the centuries, English has changed under the influence of invasions (the arrival of the Germanic tribes, the invasions of the Vikings, the Norman Conquest). The records of these changes are incomplete because we have to rely on the manuscripts that have survived from these early periods, many of which have not been fully studied.

During those times there was no agreed standard form of English. It remained as a series of different dialects that corresponded to some degree to the boundaries of the Old English kingdoms. However, by the end of the fifteenth century, Europe underwent a series of major social, political, cultural, technological and economic changes that had a profound influence on all the European languages, including English.

Standardisation

At the start of the early modern English period, Latin was seen as superior to the vernacular languages of Europe. It was a ***lingua franca***, widely used in government, education and law. For English to take its place, the language needed to undergo the process of standardisation. This meant that: a) one variety among all the existing ones had to be chosen as the standard form, b) its linguistic resources needed to be extended to make it useful for the widest range of functions, c) it needed to have internal consistency (i.e. not vary from place to place or group to group), and d) it needed to be widely available in printed form.

It is important to remember that **Standard English** is an abstract umbrella term, which covers a range of varieties that undergo change over time under the same influences that affect all varieties of English. Under the umbrella you can include Standard British English, Standard American English, Standard Australian English and all the **prestige forms** where English is spoken as a first or main language.

> **Key terms**
> - *lingua franca*
> - **Standard English**
> - prestige form

Activity 4

The text on page 14 is from William Caxton's introduction to *Eneydos*, one of the earliest texts to be printed in England.

1 What central problem, according to Caxton, does English present to a printer?

2 He discusses the problems caused by the use of two words for 'egg'. Early uses of both forms are given in the *Oxford English Dictionary*:

> The **eiren** of edderes thei to-breeken (Isiah 59:5, Wycliff)
>
> Many other briddes Hudden ... her **egges** ... In mareys
> (Piers Plowman, Langland)

Wycliff lived and worked in Yorkshire. Langland probably grew up in Oxfordshire and lived in London as an adult. What does this information suggest to you about the origins of Standard English?

3 What differences can you identify between Caxton's English and modern standard British English in:

a graphology

b lexis

c grammar.

Writing in the exam

You need to describe language using grammatical terminology where it is relevant so that you can analyse, explain and relate the features you identify to their context – language over time, the situational context or genre.

Text A: from the Preface to *Eneydos* by William Caxton (1490)

... my lorde abbot of weſtmynſter ded do ſhew me late, certayn euydences wryton in olde englysshe, for to reduce it in to our englyſſhe now vſid. And certaynly it was wreton in ſuche wyſe that it was more lyke to dutche than englyſſhe; i coude not reduce ne brynge it to be vnderſtonden. And certaynly our langage now vſed varyeth

5 ferre from that whiche was vſed and ſpoken whan I was borne. For we englyſhe men ben borne vnder the domynacyon of the mone, which is never ſtedfaſt but euer wauerynge, wexynge one ſeaſon and waneth & dyſcreaſeth another ſeaſon. And that comyn Englyſſhe that is ſpoken in one ſhyre varyeth from a nother. In ſo moche that in my days happened that certain marchauntes were in a ſhippe in Tamyſe for

10 to haue ſayled ouer the ſee into zelande, and for lacke of wynde thei taryed atte forlond, and wente to lande for to refreſh them. And one of thym named ſheffelde, a mercer, cam in to an hows and axed for mete, and ſpecyally he axyd after 'eggys'. And the good wyf anſwered that he coude ſpeke no frenſhe. And the marchaunt was angry, for he alſo coude ſpeke no frenſhe, but wolde haue egges, and ſhe vndertood

15 him not. And thenne at laſt a nother ſayd that he wolde haue 'eyren'. Then the good wyf ſayd that she vnderſtood hym wel. loo! what ſholde a man in thyſe dayes now wryte, 'egges' or 'eyren'? certaynly, it is harde to playſe euery man by cauſe of dyuersite & change of langage.

The influence of Caxton is clearly fundamentally important in the selection of the variety that became Standard English. Caxton chose the dialect he used himself, the South East Midlands and London dialect, which was use in Oxford and Cambridge, the major centres of learning, as well as in London, the centre of government.

The extension of English

The developments in learning during the Renaissance led to rapid changes in English. Interest in the classical languages and literature, and developments in the fields of science, medicine, travel and the arts meant that the existing vocabulary of English was woefully inadequate for the work it had to do. Some estimates suggest that over 30,000 new words were added to English vocabulary during this period.

Activity 5

1 The following words came into the language during the Renaissance period. Working in groups, identify:

a words that have not survived to the present day. Can you think of a reason why?

b the origins of the remaining words. Can you think of any way of classifying these words by their origins? Make a list based on the routes via which words came into the English language. Which of these routes are still used for the expansion of English vocabulary today?

alligator	alloy	bamboo	caravan	catastrophe	chocolate
counterstroke	demit	disadorn	easel	endear	expede
gloomy	grotto	invite	laugh	lottery	pincushion
potato	rouble	sago	violin	wampum	

The development of scientific writing

Changes in society in the 16th century meant that science began to emerge as an academic subject. Latin was the scientific *lingua franca* of Europe, but this meant that scientific texts were only accessible to an educated elite. Science books began to be written in the national languages of the writers, and this was to cause further expansion and changes in the language both in vocabulary, as specialist terms were developed, and in syntax, as the need for a clear, less ornate style was identified. Once again, the process of standardisation was enhanced.

Activity 6

Below are two scientific texts. Text A is taken from Robert Hook's *Micrographia*, published in 1665. Text B is a later version of Hook's work, published in 1745.

1 In what ways does the vocabulary of these texts change between 1665 and 1745?

2 Why do you think these changes have taken place?

3 How has the syntax changed from the earliest text to the latest one?

4 How does the way the audience is addressed change over time? Why?

5 Compare these texts with the modern scientific text in activity 2. What similarities and differences can you identify?

Text A

This is the appearance of a piece of very fine Taffety-riband in the bigger magnifying Glafs, which you fee exhibits it like a very convenient
5 fubftance to make Bed-mattes, or Door-matts of, or to ferve for Bee-hives, Corn-fcuttles, Chairs, or Corn-tubs, it being not unlike that kind of work, wherewith in many
10 parts in *England*, they make fuch Utenfils of Straw, a little wreathed, and bound together with thongs of Brambles. For in this Contexture, each little filament, fiber, or clew
15 of the Silk-worm, feem'd about the bignefs of an ordinary Straw, as appears by the little irregular pieces, a b, c d, and e f.

Text B

This object was a Sixpenny broad Ribbon, whose Substance viewed through the larger Magnifying-Glafs appeared like Matting for
5 Doors, or such Bafket-Work as they make in some Parts of *England*, for Bee-Hives, etc. With Straws a little wreathed or twifted: for every Filament of the Silk (several
10 whereof go to the forming of one Thread) feemed about the fize of a common Straw, as the little irregular Pieces a b, c d, e f, fhew.

The study of language: dictionaries and grammars

A standard language needs internal consistency. For the first time, English became a focus of academic study. It was taught in schools and notions of correctness began to enter the equation. One of the earliest grammars of English was William Lily's *A Shorte Introduction of Grammar*. This was based largely on Latin, but was very influential at the time and was still in use in schools in the 19th century.

Activity 7

Text A below is Lily's introduction to *A Shorte Introduction of Grammar*.

1 For whom is Lily writing in your opinion?

2 How useful do you find Lily's grammatical descriptions of English nouns?

3 Compare Lily's text with Text B, from a modern grammar aimed at a non-specialist audience of teachers. What differences can you identify between Lily's English and modern Standard British English in the key constituents of graphology, morphology, lexis, syntax and discourse?

Text A

An Introduction of the

Numbers of Nouns.

IN Nouns be two numbers, the Singular and the Plural. The singular number speaketh but of one: as, Lapis, *a stone*. The plural number speaketh of more than one: as, Lapides, *stones*.

Cases of Nouns.

NOuns be declined with six cases, Singularly, and Plurally: the Nominative, the Genitive, the Dative, the Accusative, the Vocative and the Ablative.

Nominitive cale. The Nominative case cometh before the Verb, and answereth to this question, who, or what? as, Magister docet, *The Master teacheth*.

Genitive. The Genitive case is known by this token Of: and answereth to this question whose or whereof? as, Doctrina Magistri, *The learning of the Master*.

Dative. The Dative case is known by this token To: and answereth to this question, to whom, or to what? as, Do librum Magistro, *I give a book to the Master*.

Accusative. The Accusative case followeth the Verb, and answereth to this question, whom or what? as, Amo Magistrum, *I love the Master*.

Vocative. The Vocative case is known by calling or speaking to: as, O Magister, *O Master*.

Ablative. The Ablative case is commonly joyned with Prepositions serving to the Ablative case: as, De Magistro, Of *the Master*. Coram Magistro, Before *the Master*.

Also In, With, Through, For, From, By, and Than, after the Comparative degree, be signs of the Ablative case.

1 These Articles used in declining of Nouns even in *Cicero's* time are rejected by *Vossius*, as having been introduced by Grammarians, without any sufficient reason. 2 A *Gender* being nothing else but the distinction of *lex*; there are in nature but two, the *Masculine* and the *Feminine*; and the Oriental tongues acknowledge no more. For the *Neuter*, (which the *Greeks* and *Latines* introduced with very good reason, both for variety and the better distinction of words) is not properly a new gender, but a negation of the other two, which by nature agrees to all words, whose signification includes not a distinction of sex. Though the *Greeks* and the *Latines* reserved to themselves a liberty of using many words, that were really Neuters (that is, of no sex) after the manner of using Masculines and Feminines: and others after

ter

Text B: from *English Knowledge for Secondary Teachers* by Alison Ross

Form

Another way of identifying nouns is based on their form. Nouns can change their form to indicate singular or plural. Another change in form indicates possession. Pupils can use their knowledge of morphology to identify the types of suffix that can be added to nouns. Awareness of the close connection between determiners and nouns can be consolidated in such activities.

5

Activity 8

Working in groups, imagine that you have the job of writing the first dictionary of a language.

1 How would you go about this task?

   a How would you decide which words to include and which to exclude?

   b How would you identify definitions? How would you decide whether these are accurate? What would make a definition 'correct' and what would make it 'incorrect'?

2 Read the definitions of the word 'mother' from three early dictionaries.

   a How do these entries compare with the entries for the word in a modern dictionary?

   b Can you find evidence of the earlier definitions in a modern dictionary?

Text A: from *The English Dictionarie: or, An Interpreter of hard English Words* by Henry Cockram (1623)

Mother. A disease in women when the wombe riseth with paine upwards, sweet smelles are ill for it, but loathsome savors good.

Text B: from *An English Dictionary, Explaining the Difficult Terms that are used in Divinity, Husbandry, Physick, Philosophy, Law, Navigation, Mathematicks, and other Arts and Sciences* by Elisha Coles (1676)

Mother, a painful rising of the womb, for which all sweet smells are bad, and stinking ones good.

Motherwort, Cardiaca, A cleasing (sic) Astringent herb

Mother-tongues, having no Affinity with one another

Text C: from *Gazophylacium Anglicanum*, anon (1687)

Mother from the AS Moðor, the Fr. Th. Mudder, the Belg. Moeder, or the Teut.

Mutter, the same; all from the Lat. Mater, or the Gr. Meter, idem.

Activity 9

In groups, discuss the question: Can any paper dictionary truly represent the lexicon of a language? You might consider whether such dictionaries can include recent additions to the language or all the words in a language. Can you decide on a solution to these problems?

Listen to Erin McKean talking about the problems with paper dictionaries on TED. com – www.ted.com/index.php/talks/erin_mckean_redefines_the_dictionary.html

Do you agree with her that modern paper dictionaries have what she calls a 'ham-butt' problem? Was this a problem for the writers of early dictionaries? Can any paper dictionary truly represent the lexicon of a language?

Technological change

The developments in learning that followed on from the Renaissance led to technological changes that have been ongoing. You have already seen the impact printing had on the English language. Other technological changes have also had significant effects. This section tracks one technological change – electronic communication – and the effects it has had on the English language.

We live in a world of instant news. There are hundreds of news channels on TV and radio offering instant access to what is happening around the world. It is easy to forget that simple communication over distance is a relatively recent development, and that news frequently used to take days or even weeks to arrive from its source.

The first electronic form of communication was the telegraph. There had been experiments with electronic signalling as early as 1759, but the first viable commercial system was invented in Britain and America in 1837. The first international links were established in 1865. The telegraph allowed for the transmission of written language via coded signals and was instrumental in establishing English as a global *lingua franca* for news, trade and technology.

Independent research

You can read more abourt the telegraph and its influence on the spread of English in the world of business and finance in *Changing English*, Graddol *et al.*

Please write the Name and Address of the sender, **IF NOT TO BE TELEGRAPHED**, on the back of this form.

Activity 10

In April 1912, the *SS Carpathia* transmitted a telegram from the north Atlantic to the New York offices of the White Star Line:

```
Deeply regret advise you Titanic sunk this morning
fifteenth after collision iceberg resulting serious
loss life further particulars later.
```

Because sending telegrams was time consuming (and, at a commercial level, people had to pay by the word), they developed their own style, just like text messages have. A story from the early days of telegraphy tells of a telegram sent to the writer Mark Twain by his publisher: 'Need two-page story in two days.' Twain's reply was: 'No can do two pages in two days. Can do 30 pages in two days. Need 30 days to do two pages.'

Using appropriate lexical and grammatical terminology associated with the key constituents of language, explore what characterises these example of early long-distance communication.

Activity 11

Look up the etymology and dates of the first use of the following words and phrases. When did they come into the English language? Has their meaning changed over time?

| wireless | by wire | crossed wires | telegraph |

Activity 12

1 Compare the language of telegrams with the ways in which text messages are written.

2 Why are some text messages shortened and abbreviated?

Activity 13

1 The texts below represent two early uses of the word 'computer'. What meaning did this word have when these texts were written?

2 Using dictionaries (ideally the *Oxford English Dictionary*) trace the uses of the word 'computer' to the present day.

3 What other words relating to the development of mechanical and electronic computing can you identify?

4 What social changes are suggested by the words 'blog', 'podcast', 'webpage'?

Text A: from *Exercitations on the Epistle of the Hebrews* by John Owen (1688)

<Daniel> was not a Computer of the time but a Seer as though the Question were about the way and means whereby we attain a just computation of the time, and not about the
5 thing it self. Daniel received the knowledge of this time by Revelation, as he did the time of the accomplishment of the Captivity, though he made use of the computation of time limited in the Prophecy of Jeremiah; but in
10 both he gives us a perfect Calculation of the time, and so cannot be exempted from the Talmudical Malediction.

Text B: from *The Tale of a Tub* by Jonathan Swift (1704)

Now the method of growing wise, learned, and sublime having become so regular an affair, and so established in all its forms, the number of writers must needs have increased accordingly, and to a pitch that has made it
5 of absolute necessity for them to interfere continually with each other. Besides, it is reckoned that there is not at this present a sufficient quantity of new matter left in Nature to furnish and adorn any one particular subject to the extent of a volume. This I am told by a very skilful
10 computer, who hath given a full demonstration of it from rules of arithmetic.

Activity 14

1 In groups, think of another area of technological change, for example in farming and agriculture, medicine, manufacturing, etc.

2 Identify some texts relating to your chosen area and study the ways the language relating to this area have changed over time.

3 How far have these changes moved from the specialist area into the general language of the English speaking community?

English through time: snapshots of British English

In this sub-section, you will look at examples of English written for different purposes and in different contexts across a wide time scale.
Working in groups, read Texts A–J carefully.

Writing in the exam

Remember when you are analysing data in the exam, it isn't enough to list the features you find (sometimes known as feature counting). You must identify the features that are relevant to the question, discuss how they relate to the context of the text and identify any patterns that relate to the overall topic of the question.

Activity 15

1 Identify ways the language has changed across the key constituents of graphology, morphology, lexis and grammar.

2 Discuss the discourse of the texts. How are they structured for their tenor and mode? How do they address their audience? How do they refer to themselves? How does the semantic field relate to language choices? Can you identify differences in these key concepts across time?

3 Can you suggest reasons why these changes might have taken place?

The language of advice

Text A: From *Your Pocket Guide to Sex* by Nick Fisher (1994)

Maybe you're already having sex which is perfect. It might be so brilliant, that you just haven't got time to read this book. Fair enough. Good on you.

But most of us aren't having perfect sex. Most of us have got questions
5 we'd like to ask or problems we'd like to share, but are reticent, because we don't know what's acceptable. Or we're just plain embarrassed.

Your Pocket Guide to Sex tries to prod around in the areas people have difficulty with. It tries to explain a range of facts, explode a bundle of myths, give useful contacts, describe what safer sex is and even dig up a
10 laugh or two's worth of sexual trivia.

There are quotes from people who've been there, done that, there are comments from seasoned celebrities and there's even some assorted nonsense about what we used to think, do and feel about sex in Ancient Times.

15 There are lots of things we didn't include. For example, there's no a–z of 101 new sexual positions. This is a book about getting to know yourself, your partners and safely enjoying and experimenting with the sex that you do have.

So what if you are unsure about undressing in front of someone else? So
20 what if you've never had sex and don't know where to start? Maybe you're a lot more like the rest of us than you think.

With a bit of luck, Your Pocket Guide to Sex might help you understand the complexities of sex, be aware of the dangers, feel more confident in yourself
25 and realise that good relations and emotions can count for a lot more than notches on the bed post.

Text B: from *Instructions to his Sonne: and to Posteritie* by Sir Walter Raleigh (published 1632, but written between 1603 and 1618)

The next, and greatest care in this life, ought to be in choice of thy Wife, and the onely danger therin is Beautie, by which all men in all Ages, wise and foolish, have beene betrayed. And though I know it vaine to use Reasons, or Arguments to dismay thee, from being captivated therewith, there being few that ever resisted the

5 Witcherie; yet I cannot omit to warne thee, as of other things, which may be thy destruction for the present time. It is true, that every man preferreth his fantasie in that Appetite before all other worldly desires, leaving the care of Honour, credit, and safetie in respect thereof; yut remember, though these afflictions doe not last, yet the bonds of Marriage dureth to the end of thy life; and therefore better to be

10 borne withall in a Mistris, then in a wife; for when thy humour shal change thou art yet free to chuse again (if thou give thy selfe that vaine liberty.) Remember, secondly, that if thou marry for Beauty, thou bindest thy selfe for all thy life for that which perchance will neither last nor please thee one yeere; and when thou hast it, it will bee unto thee of no price at all, for the desire dyeth when it is attayned, and the

15 affection perisheth, when it is satisfied. Remember when thou wert a sucking Child, that thou diddest love thy Nurse, and that thou wert fond of her, after a while thou didst love thy dry Nurse, and didst forget the other, after thet thou didst also despise her; so will it be with thee in thy liking in elder yeeres; and therefore, though thou canst not forbeare to love, yet forbeare to linke, and after a while thou shalt find an

20 alteration in thy selfe, and see another far more pleasing then the first, second or third love ... Let thy time of marriage bee in thy young and strong yeeres; for beleeve it, ever the young Wife betrayeth the old Husband, and shee that had thee not in thy flower, will despise thee in thy fall, and thou shalt bee unto her, but a captivity and sorrow. Thy best time will be towards thirty, for as the younger times are unfit, either

25 to chuse or to governe a Wife and family; so if thou stay long, thou shalt hardly see the education of thy Children, which being left to strangers, are in effect lost, and better were it to be unborne then ill-bred; for thereby thy posterity shall either perish, or remaine a shame to thy name, and family.

The language of personal communication

Text C: from a letter written by Margaret Paston to her husband John in 1441, right at the start of the early modern English period

To my ryth reuerent and worscheful husbond John Paston.

Ryth reuerent and worscheful husbond, I recomaunde me to yow, desyryng hertyly to here of yowre wylfare, thankyng yow for þe tokyn þat ye sent me be Edmunde Perys, preyng yow to wete þat my modyr sent to my fadyr to London for a govne

5 cloth of mvstyrddevyllers to make of a govne for me; and he tolde my modyr and me wanne he was comme hom þat he cargeyt yow to bey it aftyr þat he were come ovte of London. I pre yow, yf it be not bowt, þat ye wyl wechesaf to by it and send yt hom as sone as ye may, for I haue no govne to werre þis wyntyr but my blake and my grene a Lyere, and þat ys so comerus þat I ham wery to wer yt.

Glossary

wete – know, be aware of

govne – gown

mvstyrddevyllers – grey woollen cloth from Mouster de Villers in Normandy

wechesaf (vouchsafe) – promise

lyere – black and green woollen cloth from Lierre near Antwerp

Text D: from a letter sent to a personal friend (2008)

Happy Birthday!!

I hope this year's birthday will be a happy & memorable one for you. You will certainly be in my thoughts. Thank you for the money I received September 24th! With the holidays coming up, it will go toward the
5   holiday treats commissary has each year. I hope they have a good variety.

I'm doing okay & my family are all doing well. Dad & Russ came to see me last month & we had a really nice visit! I always enjoy my time with them. He killed a great big Timber rattle snake up at their cabin. It was
10   coiled-up right next to their steps.

Enclosed is a letter I wrote for my step-niece Heather. She is a clinical director over two youth homes for troubled teens with sexual problems. She asked if I would write a letter for them. She said my letter to them has had a positive impact. I hope it will have a 'lasting'
15   impact on them!

Summer, my attorney, is coming tomorrow to see me. I'm really looking forward to seeing her. She & I get along very well. Things look VERY GOOD for me. My other attorney is in Panama & will be back sometime next week. He's an awesome guy!

Text E: a text message

MISSED U TODAY. HOPE U HAD A GOOD MEETING. REMBER TO PICK UP SPUDS ON YR WAY HOME. LV J XX

The language of instructional texts

Text F: from *The Accomplished Cook* by Robert May (1660)

To make Cream Tarts

Thicken cream with muskefield bisket bread, and serve it in a dish, stick wafers round about it, and slices of preserved citteron, and in the middle a preserved orange with biskets, the garnish of the dish being of puff-paste.

5   Or you may boil quinces, warden peas, and pippins in slices or quarters, and strain them into cream, as also these fruits, melacattons, necturnes, apricocks, peaches, plums, or cherries, and make your tarts of these forms.

Text G: from *BBC Good Food Magazine* (2008)

Berry Slump

Serves 4–6 • Prep 10 mins • COOK 30 mins • Easy

100g/4oz butter, softened, plus extra for greasing
100g/4oz castor sugar, plus 2 tbsp extra
100g/4oz self-raising flour
2 eggs
1 tbsp milk
2 tsp vanilla extract
600g/1lb 5oz frozen mixed summer berries
25g/1oz flaked almonds

1. In a food processor, whizz together the butter, 100g sugar, flour, eggs, milk and 1 tsp vanilla extract until smooth. Lightly grease an oval 20 x 30cm baking dish or 20cm deep cake tin, then tip in the frozen fruit. Scatter over the remaining sugar and vanilla extract. Dollop over the cake mix, then smooth all over with the back of a spoon to cover the fruit. Make a little dip in the middle of the mixture to ensure it cooks evenly throughout. Scatter over the almonds.

2. Heat oven to 180°C/fan 160°C/gas 4. Cook for 45 min until the fruit is hot and the sponge is cooked through. Serve warm with custard or vanilla ice cream.

Text H: from *Mrs Beeton's Book of Household Management* (1861)

CLEAR ASPARAGUS SOUP

(*Fr.*- Potage aux Pointes d' Asperges)

Ingredients. — 5 lbs. of lean beef, 3 slices of bacon, ½ pint of ale, a few leaves of white beet, spinach, 1 cabbage lettuce, a little mint, sorrel, and marjoram, a pint of asparagus-tops, cut small, the crust of 1 French roll, seasoning to taste, 2 quarts of water.

Mode. — Put the beef, cut into pieces and rolled in flour into a stewpan, with the bacon at the bottom ; cover it close, and set it on a slow fire, stirring it now and then till the gravy is drawn. Put in the water and ale, and season to taste with pepper and salt, and let it stew gently for 2 hours; then strain the liquor, and take off the fat, and add the white beet, spinach, cabbage lettuce and mint, sorrel and sweet marjoram, pounded. Let these boil up in the liquor, then put in the asparagus-tops, cut small, and allow them to boil until all is tender. Serve hot, with the crust of the French roll cut into small rounds or squares in the dish.

Time. – Altogether 3 hours.

Average cost, per quart, *3s*

Seasonable from May to August

Sufficient for 8 persons

The language of reporting legal cases

Text I: from the Ordinary's accounts (1726)
The Ordinary of Newgate was the prison chaplain, whose duty it was to provide spiritual care to prisoners condemned to death. One of the perks of his job was the right to publish the prisoner's final confession together with an account of his life which made the Ordinary around £200 per annum. See www.oldbaileyonline.org. ref. no. OA172260509

The
ORDINARY *of* NEWGATE *his* ACCOUNT,
Of the Behaviour, Confession, and dying Words of the Male-factors, who were Executed on *Monday*, the 9th of this Instant *May*, 1726, at *Tyburn*.

While under Sentence, they were instructed in the Principles of our Holy Christian Religion; in the Original of Right and Property; they were taught the great Evil of the Sin of Murder from several weighty Considerations; and if Murder in general be one of the most heinous Sins, then in proportion the murderer of one's nearest and dearest Relation must be still a greater Sin than common Murder; and not only of one who is most nearly Related, but also who, by the Laws of God and Man, is a superiour Person in Power and Honour; for that the Husband is called the Head of the Wife, her Lord, &c. and therefore the Laws of this Kingdom have wisely declar'd it to be a greater Crime, and affix'd a severer Punishment upon a Wife's murdering her Husband, than upon other Murderers, &c. I likewise insisted upon the Villany and Uncleanness of unnatural Sins, which ought not to be nam'd among People who have any remainders of Civility lest, much less among Christians who profess the true Religion, teaching us to deny all Ungodliness and Worldly Lusts &c especially the Lusts of the Flesh, &c. I show'd 'em the Evil of this Sin from God's visible Judgments inflicted on Sodom and Gomorrah, and the neighbouring Cities, in raining Fire and Brimstone from Heaven upon them, and consuming them as in a Moment, &c,

And in the Apostle St Paul, Rom. 1. and St. Jude in his Epistle, inveighing so much against these most impious and notorious Sinners, &c.

In time of delivering these and many other useful Instructions, all of them appeared to be attentive; but no outward Signs of Repentance and Sorrow for Sin, requisite in every sincere Christian, much more in such notable and most impious Offenders, as many, if not all of 'em were; Wood the Murderer was most affected, but he appeared but 2 or 3 Days in Chapel, for falling sick, he died in the Condemn'd Hold a few Days before the Sentence was put in Execution; Billings, who actually murder'd Mr. Hayes, by one stroke of a Hatchet in the hind-part of his Head, was a confus'd, hard-hearted young Fellow, and had few external Signs of Penitence; Mrs. Hayes was too unconcerned, and I fear too often her Mind was taken up with things altogether foreign to the Purpose, and great Work which she had then upon hand; Gillingham, Map, and the rest of 'em were attentive and comply'd with the Worship, excepting one who was a Roman Catholick.licit sympathy and divert attention away from the issue of personal responsibility for a crime.

Text J: from *The Times*, 19 September 2007
PHIL SPECTOR MURDER TRIAL
JURY UNABLE TO REACH A VERDICT
— *Chris Ayres in Los Angeles* —

Jurors in the murder trial of Phil Spector last night told the judge that they had reached an impasse in their deliberations, raising the prospect of a mistrial being called as soon as today.

A mistrial would essentially leave the wildly eccentric music producer a free man.

At a hearing at Los Angeles Superior Court, Judge Larry Paul Fidler questioned the jurors, who told him that they were split 7 to 5 — a sign of irreconcilable differences. They did not reveal which way the balance tipped: guilty or not guilty.

When asked if they could reach a decision if they were allowed to convict Mr Spector of involuntary manslaughter, instead of the original charge of second-

degree murder, only three jurors said yes. Analysts said that this did not bode well for the prosecution.

Mr Spector, 67, is accused of picking up Lana Clarkson, a struggling actress who was working as a cocktail waitress at the House of Blues, on a February night in 2003, taking her home to his Los Angeles "castle", and shooting her in the face.

The creator of the "Wall of Sound" technique of the Sixties, and a one-time producer for The Beatles, had been known for decades in the music industry for his drunken gunplay.

Nevertheless, there were no eyewitnesses to the shooting — aside from perhaps Mr Spector, who did not testify — and over the six months of the trial prosecutors struggled to prove, using blood spatter analysis, dental fragments and gunshot residue, that Ms Clarkson could not have shot herself or that the gun could not have gone off by accident.

Ms Clarkson's alleged depression, debt, chronic pain and her personal diary — in which she threatened to kill herself only weeks before the shooting — also worked against the prosecution. She was also found to have forged letters of recommendation from TV executives, possibly in an effort to borrow more money from a wealthy friend.

At just after 3pm yesterday, the jurors were sent home to "recharge" overnight. Mr Spector, meanwhile, had spent the afternoon in a pinstripe suit and red tie, hanging around the court with an entourage of 16 people, including his lawyers, jury consultants, private investigators, interns, relatives and bodyguards.

Ms Clarkson's mother, Donna Clarkson, was also present, along with one of the alleged victim's best friends, Nili Hudson.

A mistrial would force the prosecution to decide if it wanted to spend several million more dollars of taxpayers' money to try a second time to convict Mr Spector. With public opinion against Mr Spector, a mistrial would probably be considered yet another celebrity debacle, the first being the acquittal of O. J. Simpson 12 years ago on double-murder charges.

Many Americans believe that defendants with multimillion dollar defence teams can convince jurors that "beyond reasonable doubt" means beyond all scientific doubt.

Mr Spector has previously claimed that Ms Clarkson, who was 41 when she died, "kissed the gun". The prosecutors countered by calling as witnesses several of Mr Spector's former girlfriends, who all said that they had previously been threatened at gunpoint by him.

The jurors will meet again today.

Independent research

Original texts giving details of criminal trials, court proceedings and information about the lives of prisoners from 1674–1913 can be found on www. oldbaileyonline.org/. This website is a useful resource for studying language change and contains interesting data for a Unit 4 language investigation.

Social and cultural change

You have looked at the development of English as a national language (see page 12) and the development of a standard form (p 13). Standard English is often seen as a superior or higher form of the language, and is often (as in this book) used as a base form against which other varieties are compared.

Regional variation

The development of English as a national language and the emergence of an agreed standard did not reduce variation in English across the British Isles. For example, the language of northern England is different from the language of South East England. The language of the West Country is different again.

Regional variation has also undergone major changes over the years. The Industrial Revolution brought communities into urban environments, and since then rural communities have declined and more people live in cities that ever before. Other patterns of social change have led to the mixing of people speaking mutually intelligible dialects, which has led to the formation of new dialects. This process is sometimes called **koineization**, and the new dialect formed this way is referred to as a **koiné language**.

Because much language change takes place unobserved, this process has not often been studied. There seem to be two main scenarios in which this kind of dialect formation takes place: the settlement of a relatively large territory in which a previous population is ousted or assimilated, and the formation of a new town within a defined geographical boundary. Examples of the former are the settlement of New Zealand, largely by English speakers in the nineteenth century (see page 29). An example of the latter is the establishment of the new town of Milton Keynes. You can listen to students at Milton Keynes College on http://www.youtube.com/user/MKcollege1 search for 'MK6' video or 'Computing & IT'.

Key terms

- **koineization**
- **koiné language**

Independent research

Read about dialect mixing and the development of new dialects in papers by Paul Kerswill on www.ling.lancs.ac.uk/profiles/Paul-Kerswill/.

Activity 16

Texts A–C below represent examples of English spoken by people in different regions of the UK. Accent is not indicated unless the word is non-standard, in which case the pronunciation has been represented by spelling, with a phonemic transcription the first time it appears.

1 How do these regional forms differ from Standard British English in the key constituents of lexis, syntax and grammar?

2 Look up your own region on http://sounds.bl.uk and listen to any recordings you can find. Do the recordings represent the variety spoken in your region? Do they represent the language of you and your peers?

Text A: South Yorkshire man from Barnsley

Y: I mean tha's /ðaz/ got thi /ðl/ mates and tha comes down gym (0.5) I mean (.) that's what life's about in it /ɪn?ɪt/ I goes an earns some money and there's training and seeing your mates and the your lass but tha's got to go out and have a good laugh (0.5) Life's too short kid (.) tha can't worry all t /ʔ/
5   time (.) tha's gotta let thi hair down and get yersen in club and have a bit of a boogy and make a fool on thissen chatting to all t /ʔ/ nice women. And tha walks home with a bag of chips on thi own but so what (.) That's life (.) Tha's gotta go out with thi mates and have a good night (.) it doesn't matter if tha pulls a bird or not (.) tha' with thi mates and owt else is a bonus.

Text B: Geordie speaker from north-east England

I made me way down to the Central Station and got a tram the trams wor /wɔ/ running in them days. Off along Scotswood Road we gans /gænz. /Wey ye /jə/ know what the old trams wor like – they swung about like hikeys. As we got near to Clumbor Street I made me way to the stairs
5   holding the rail with one hand and the floors high above me head with the other, when suddenly she stops! I just couldn't help meself; down the stairs I came cowpin me kreels at the bottom and out I shoots onto the road. I opened me eyes and all I could see wor faces looking down, and for all the shouting nobody did nowt /naʊt/

Text C: South Yorkshire woman from Rotherham

I had this dream and I was in a car in the back of the car and there were two people that I knew in the front (.) we were driving up a hill and there were traffic lights on either side of the hill (.) and on the left-hand corner there was a pub (.) and at the top of the hill there was a big roundabout with a
5   big carpark in the middle (.) okay right (.) and on about halfway round the roundabout there was a big co-op a big big co-op (.) erm and then about a year ago just after I had the dream (.) we were going up this hill and I was in the back of the car and my mum and dad were driving (.) we were on us way to Chesterfield (.) and (.) I'd never been before but I thought I recognised
10   it (.) and then my dream came back to me (.) and I said to my mum this is strange and I had a dream where there were two traffic lights on either side and a pub (.) and there was a roundabout but in my dream there was a co-op half way round (.) and my mum said oh well that must be just a coincidence (.) and we got round the roundabout and there was a sign saying co-op but it had been sort of disguised from view before (.) and there you go'

You may have noticed that Activity 16 did not ask you to look at the key constituent phonology. An important thing to remember about Standard British English is that it has nothing to do with pronunciation. Standard British English is spoken with a range of regional accents.

So what is Standard English? As noted above, it refers to an abstract form of language that does not really exist, but it is represented by the forms Standard British English, Standard American English, etc. Some people see standard forms as formal and vernacular forms as informal, but this is not the case. Standard language is not a style. Every speaker will have a range of styles that vary according to context, and speakers may vary their style depending on how they perceive, or how they wish to establish, the context.

In the examples in Activity 16, it is reasonable to assume that none of the speakers are using the most informal style in their range because they are being interviewed and recorded. This will affect the way they speak (see Observer's paradox, Unit 4, page 132).

In fact, Standard English is a dialect. It is often described as a social dialect because it is no longer associated with a region (despite its origins in the dialect of the South East), but more with middle-class, educated social groups.

Cultural change

As you will have observed from the brief account above that English has always been influenced by contacts with other languages and other cultures. The development of English as a world language via colonialism and post-colonialism will be discussed in more detail on pages 29–41, but an important aspect of British English relates to cultural contacts.

The lexicon of English has expanded massively since the earliest days of the language. For political and historical reasons, English has borrowed words from other languages all over the world, and still does. As new cultures and concepts enter society, their influence is seen in the language by, among other things, developments in the English word stock.

Take it further

You can listen to examples of Newcastle English and South Yorkshire English on the British Library website: http://sounds.bl.uk Mark from Byker, Newcastle upon Tyne talks about getting married and Dee from Sheffield talks about running away as a teenager. The site also offers analysis of the key constituents of the varieties.

Activity 17

Read the lists A and B below. Try to locate the original source of each word in the dictionary, for example, 'bonanza' is identified as American slang, but its origins are Spanish. You may not be able to find the words in list A if your dictionary is not a very recent one, but you should be able to identify the place of origin.

List A

| anime | bada bing | barbie | desi | g-man | honcho |
| intifada | jilbab | karaoke | sushi | wok | |

List B

adobe	algebra	bonanza	carriage	contralto	dilettante
dingo	giraffe	hoosegow	jazz	juggernaut	pariah
tattoo (marking on the skin)	tobacco	voyage			

Since the 1950s people from the Indian subcontinent and the West Indies have made England their home. They brought with them the versions of English that had developed in their countries of origin as a result of colonisation and added their accents and dialects to the ones already spoken in the UK. Since they settled in urban areas, speakers of Asian and Caribbean descent have absorbed aspects of local dialects and produced new varieties often identified by such names as London Jamaican or Bradford Asian English.

Independent research

You can listen to clips of Asian and Caribbean English, as well as other audio recordings demonstrating how the sound of English has changed over the last 50 years, at www.bl.uk/learning/langlit/sounds/index.html.

Key term

- patois
- connotation

These settlers have also influenced Standard British English, giving English words like 'balti' (literally meaning 'bucket') and a whole host of other food terms. Slang, in particular, plays host to many terms originating from Asian or Caribbean languages. Terms like 'chuddies' (underpants) or 'desi' (typically Asian). Even the tag question, 'innit' is thought to owe some of its popularity to the British Caribbean or the British Asian community. In this case, it was also part of the Welsh dialect, but has its strongest associations with the Asian community.

Varieties of English associated with ethnic groups often carry a range of names. Black English, Black English vernacular, American African vernacular English are some of the terms used. In the late 1980s, Viv Edwards carried out research into the language in a black community in Dudley. She used the term the community itself used – **patois**. This term is used less now as it is seen as having negative **connotations**.

Activity 18

Read Texts A and B below.

1 Identify any differences between the English of the people who were brought up in the Caribbean and came to the UK as adults, and the speech of the young man who was born and grew up in the UK.

2 What aspects of the key constituents of language are features of these varieties?

3 What attitudes towards their language and community do the speakers show?

4 What do the different styles used by the speaker in text B suggest to you about his attitudes to his language?

5 How do these attitudes affect their language?

> **Text A:** Group of Afro-Caribbean first generation immigrants, taking about their early experiences of life in the UK
>
> Mr J: Dem tings (.) man (.) me no inna dem at all (.) sausage and pie (.) no sah
>
> Mrs S: I am not kidding some rough piece a ting I go tru inna dis very Englan
>
> 5 Mr K: First time de work-dem yuh could get de work-dem cause de work-dem was so bad nobody want dem I tell yu something I went up to dis Stalybridge here (.) man (0.5) Man (.) an yu ave dis place where dem wash de calico an is pure water (.) acid (.) chemic
>
> Mr J: I come ere an see some white women do some work (.) I wouldn't
> 10 do it
>
> <Interviewer: Why (.) what was it>
>
> Mr K: Boil the calico into it before dem set it out
>
> Mr J: Spraying man (.) with de (.) what you call it (.) de paint If yu ever see de poor woman-dem (.) I wouldn't do it at all
>
> 15 Mr K: An dem ave a ole down inna de groun about seven foot yu know (.) an yu ave to go down inna de groun (0.5) An de waste (.) everyting a run out an a come ova de machine
>
> Mr J: Mi seh if a me fe do dat (.) mi prefer I walk go ome back (.) umh-um
>
> Mr K: An all de cloth come doun inna de pit (.) yu know (.) an yu hafi
> 20 ketch-dem an twine dem round dat when dem a pull out back (.) dem no tie up An it hot (.) yu know (.) When I tell yu say it hot (.) An yu ave on a water boot or clog (.) An man when yu hear dat steam build up an dat acid and dat chemic mi she (.) sometime yu ear man bawl down dere (0.5) Yu hafi run go wid a ladda (.) yu know (0.5) An when im come up pon de ladda (.) straight tru de door im gone (.)
> 25 outadoor (0.5) An when yu go out deh (.) man (.) mi say (.) yu eye a run water (.) yu troat bitter (0.5) Sometime believe yu me (.) I don't

		know how some of de men-dem come out a dat door. I work dere
		for a little while (.) I say no sah (.) cyaant leave fi come ere fi some
30		work (.) say yu a work job (.) an yu know ow much a week (0.5)
		How much a week yu tink
	Mr J:	Seven poun
	Mr K:	Seven poun an when dem trim it down done yu get some (.) man
		get all £3.50
35	Mr J:	Tek out too much
	Mr K:	Yeah man (.) a wha do yu man

Text B: Young black man talking about a questionnaire he has just
completed for a black fieldworker, from Viv Edwards' research

<**Talking to a black researcher**>

Dem (the questions) alright in away, right. Dem reasonable. Dem coulda
be lickle better, but dem reasonable. Me na bex wid dem, dem alright …
When white people ready fi write some rubbish bout black people, dem
5 can do it, dem can do it, right. So dat's why me say dem reasonable. Notn
wrong wid dem.

<**Talking to a white interviewer**>

I say it come from Africa really. It started from dere tru slavery. Dat's di way
I see it. It started from there, yeah. But those kids what born over here
10 right, they don't want to admit it. Like Paddy, they don't want to admit it
right that our culture started from Africa.

2   Diversity in English

In Part 1 (pp 9–29) you explored how English has changed over the last 1500
years. You studied the origins of English, how it absorbed features of other
languages and how it evolved into the many different forms of the language
we use today. This is only half the story. From the Early Modern English period,
English started to spread from the geographical confines of England.

As a result, English can now be found in many different forms throughout the world:

- as the **first language** of a country. England is not the only country where
  English has status as the first language, that is the **official language** of
  a country. Amongst these are America, Australia, Canada, Jamaica, New
  Zealand and Scotland

- as a **second language**. In some countries, English has an official status, and
  newspapers and other documents are produced in English, as well as the
  'home' language. Among the many examples of countries where English has
  second-language status are India, Pakistan and Singapore

- as a *lingua franca*. A language used to allow routine communication between
  groups of people who do not share the same first language.

- as a foreign language. In this case the language will have no official status.
  Individuals decide to learn English for their own purposes.

The texts in your exam could be taken from any of these areas and could
even be from varieties you have not specifically studied. This is not a cause for
concern as you can apply the key constituents of language, which formed an
important part of your AS studies, to any form.

These 'international' forms of English often come back to the British Isles,
where our form of English is up to its old tricks – absorbing features from these
international varieties back into itself.

> **Key terms**
>
> - first language
> - official language
> - second language

American English

When people think of English on the global stage, this is the first variety that will spring to mind. This is no surprise. It has over 200 million speakers and its culture and media have saturated many parts of the globe. This makes **American English** (AmE) an important contributor to the spread of English.

History

The first permanent English settlement in America was founded in 1607 on the eastern coast of Virginia. Then, in 1620, a group of Puritans, or the 'Pilgrim Fathers' as they later became known, arrived and settled in what is now Massachusetts. By the mid-1600s, 25,000 immigrants had settled in the area.

These settlers brought their language with them – their grammar, vocabulary and pronunciation. Changes that took place in British English (BrE) after the key settlement dates are not reflected in the development of American English. This means we sometimes find American English using forms popular in Elizabethan times, for example 'fall' for 'autumn', which have since fallen from use in British English. If you used this form, people would (probably) know what you meant but would accuse you of speaking 'American'. However, 'fall' was in use in England until the 16th century. Other similar examples of British English originally used in the Early Modern English period which we would now associate with being American are 'trash' (used by Shakespeare), 'mad' for 'angry' and 'deck' of cards (British English now uses 'pack').

By 1790, the population of America had reached 4 million, with many living on the Atlantic coast. Immigration continued throughout the following decades and centuries – Germans, Italians, Irish and Jewish groups from across Europe and the Middle East, all settled in America and brought their own languages with them. These influenced the development of American English – especially the vocabulary.

Below are six word lists containing words that entered American English from Dutch, German, Irish, Italian, Spanish and Yiddish. Can you match the word list to the language they originally came from?

Key terms

- American English (AmE)

Writing in the exam

American English has a history of its own. It has only been separate from British English for 400 years; however there have been some significant changes in its formality and vocabulary even in this relatively short lifespan. Texts from the earliest period of American history can be examined in the context of a 'historical text' in a similar way to British English historical texts, as well as in an 'international English' context.

Activity 19

Below are six word lists containing words that entered American English from Dutch, German, Irish, Italian, Spanish and Yiddish. Can you match the word list to the language they originally came from?

a vamoose, stampede, ranch, corral

b smithereens, speakeasy, hooligan

c espresso, pizza, radio, macaroni

d dumb, shyster, bummer

e sleigh, coleslaw, boss, waffle

f pastrami, glitch, phooey

Although the words in Activity 19 were originally used in America, many of them entered British English soon afterwards. You will find many people complain about 'Americanisms' entering English. This is a social judgement, not a linguistic one. People are quite happy to let French words in as these are thought of as refined, but American is often thought of as boorish and unfavourable. However, such people are often unaware of the amount of American vocabulary already in the language. Few today would complain about 'teenager', 'commuter' or 'seafood', all of which originally came from America.

Vocabulary

The differences between American English and British English lexis fall into four main categories:

- same word in both American English and British English, but it has different meanings
- same word, but it has an additional meaning in one variety
- same word, but there is a difference in the level of formality, how often it is used or its connotations, for example, 'Autumn' can be used in American English, but is considered to be very formal
- same concept, but different words are used in American English and British English.

It is the final area that is most likely to cause misunderstanding between users. The following extract comes from a Wikipedia biography of the American current affairs presenter, Larry King.

> He said that he tries to project an image of earnestness and sincerity in each interview, and the format of the show (King in *suspenders* instead of suit and tie, sitting directly next to the guest) reinforces that.
>
> http://en.wikipedia.org/wiki/Larry_King_Live

To any British English user this is quite funny. It makes us think he is in women's underwear. In American English, 'suspender' means 'braces' (their term for the item of underwear is 'garter belt').

Technological advances like the Internet have increased awareness of many items of American English vocabulary to the point where we are barely aware of the differences. Despite this, we still do not tend to use significant quantities of American English vocabulary where there is an British English alternative available.

The pronunciation of American English

Perhaps the most interesting aspect of pronunciation rests not in any of the sound differences but in the fact there is no American equivalent of **Received Pronunciation** (RP). The majority variety is known as **General American** (GA), which does not carry the same social class associations.

You can explore the sound of American English (and of English spoken in several other parts of the globe) at http://accent.gmu.edu/howto.php. This site has audio files and IPA transcripts of different speakers reading the same sentence. Listen to several different American accents and plot some of the key differences.

Trudgill and Hannah's *International English* has a very detailed section on the phonology of American English, including detail on regional variation. See Chapter 3, pages 35–55. For a more entertaining look at features of American pronunciation without all the IPA, look at Chapter 7 in Bill Bryson's *Mother Tongue*.

Orthography

At the level of written language, it is the orthography that often strikes the British English user as a major source of variation. Spelling variation can be traced back to Noah Webster who produced the *American Spelling Book* in 1783. Initially, Webster followed the norms established by Dr Johnson and he opposed reform. By 1804, he had changed his mind and, in a revised version, he proposed several reforms. These included deleting the 'u' from '-our' endings and dropping the '-k' from words ending '-ick' such as 'magick' (something that British English eventually followed). Such reforms were not just about spelling. They were also about creating a distinct linguistic identity for the people of American – as Webster himself stated.

Independent research

Read Chapter 11 of Bill Bryson's *Mother Tongue* for a more in-depth exploration of lexical issues and find out how an American saved the English from 'gyratory circuses'.

Larry King wearing a rather fetching pair of suspenders

Key terms

- **Received Pronunciation (RP)**
- **General American (GA)**

Read more about the non-systematic spelling differences between American English and British English in David Crystal's *Encyclopedia of the English Language*, pages 80–81 and 307. Chapter 13 of Melvyn Bragg's *The Adventure of English* also discusses the influence of Noah Webster's dictionary and the American love of the 'spelling bee'.

You will not be expected to have a full knowledge of the AmE phonological system. Instead you will have to describe the features exhibited in the text and to identify patterns. You should try to be familiar with the sounds of RP and the **International Phonetic Alphabet** (IPA), as well as relevant terminology for describing speech sounds. Phonology can be discussed in written texts if there is an attempt to represent accent through **orthography**. If this is the case, you will have to relate the orthography to the phonology using IPA symbols and terminology associated with speech sounds, where appropriate.

Grammar

There are few significant differences between Standard British English and American English – especially at the level of educated speech. At the level of colloquial and dialectal grammar, the variations can be as wide as those found in the British Isles, and cannot be described here, but even these will follow patterns British English users can follow. It is after all, the same language (well, except in cases like 'Pennsylvania Dutch', spoken by approximately 30,000 Amish, who use English vocabulary with German syntax, giving forms like 'outen the light'!).

Some of the features have interesting links back to change over time. This is because the grammatical differences tend to originate from the two varieties developing at different rates.

Most American English grammar is perfectly understandable to the British English user – but it may not be Standard British English. Very careful reading of American texts is needed if you wish to comment on the grammar. Many features of Standard American English are used by British English users while the Standard British English forms may be rarely used.

<aside>
Key terms

• International Phonetic Alphabet (IPA)

• orthography
</aside>

<aside>
Writing in the exam

To meet the Assessment objectives, you must remember to relate comments on grammar to the context and make links to the construction of meaning, as well as any relevant theories and research.
</aside>

<aside>
Take it further

Trudgill and Hannah's book *International English* contains an extensive and detailed section on American grammar and details many of the subtle differences. Read pages 55–79. Are you always familiar with the Standard British English forms? What does this tell you about Standard English and its users?
</aside>

Activity 20

The following examples all come from the Corpus of Contemporary American English (http://www.americancorpus.org/).

1 Identify any differences in these examples between American English and British English.

2 Can you classify the differences into key constituents of language?

a There is no alternative. No alternative. Peace talks haven't gotten anywhere.

b Then it came to him he had better swim for the bottom. When he dove down, he felt Bantry come loose from him, and he kept going down.

c I am available Monday through Friday for consultation.

d It is five after seven.

e I haven't seen Rachel in ages.

f I looked out the window.

g The shed is in back of the building.

h Each subject was then given a half pound of M&Ms; so that actual consumption could also be measured.

i He was real skinny, didn't look like he does now, huh?

j We're going to go to your calls momentarily, but I want to get the thoughts of each on the scenario, what they think would be a good idea to do from here.

African American Vernacular English

This dialect of American English has been attracting a great deal of linguistic and political attention and no section on American English would be complete without some reference. The association of rap and hip-hop (and all their sub-varieties) with this dialect means it is common in the media and some of its language features are entering the mainstream. It is important to note that not all black Americans speak **African American Vernacular English** (AAVE) and not all of its speakers are black.

Activity 21

Find an example of some authentic African American Vernacular English. You can find such data in media such as television, radio, blogs or YouTube videos (a particularly good source can be audience-based chat shows and interviews with certain music personalities). Can you find examples of the key features of African American Vernacular English phonology and grammar?

Australian English

Like American English, there is very little regional variation in grammar and vocabulary in **Australian English** (AusE). While there are some grammatical differences when compared to British English, the majority of variation is phonological and lexical. Until quite recently RP was the **prestige accent**, so at the top of the social scale we find accents close to RP.

David Crystal, in *The English Language*, estimates that about 10% of the population have accents close to RP, with 30% showing 'broad' Australian. In between we find a similar situation to American English with **General Australian**. General Australian has much in common with the London accent.

Activity 22

1 Think of any reasons why the Australian accent has elements in common with the London accent.

2 English has been in Australia since 1778. Explain why we might find less variation at all levels than is apparent in American English.

Phonology

G'day mates!

The pronunciation of this stereotypical Australian greeting illustrates one of the most widely noticed aspects of Australian English phonology. Australians make little distinction between the dipthongs /ɑɪ/ and /eɪ/. Such lack of distinction can make some words, such as 'main' and 'mine' near **homophones**.

- Like RP, Australian English uses a long vowel in words like 'bath' and 'palm', but the vowel is further forward in the mouth so /ɑː/ rather than RP /æ/. However, unlike RP and more like northern varieties of British English, the short /æ/ is found in words where the vowel is followed by a **nasal** plus another consonant as in 'plant' and 'chance'. There is, however, some regional variation in this feature.

- There is frequently an additional /ə/ before final nasal consonants, for example 'film' and 'known' become /filəm/ and /nəuən/ (also a feature of some British English accents).

Key terms

- homophone
- nasal
- Australian Questioning Intonation (AQI)/ High Rising Terminals (HRT)

Recently another feature has become one of the most defining aspects of Australian phonology and one which has successfully colonised some forms of British English – the **Australian Questioning Intonation** (AQI), also commonly known as **High Rising Terminals** (HRT). This term refers to the use of rising intonation on the end of *statements* rather than questions. Its function is to confirm that the other party is listening and understands what is being said.

My favourite Australian musician is Nick Cave.	I saw him play at sunset at Glastonbury.

Grammar

As far as written language is concerned, it is almost impossible to tell if a text has been written in Australian or British English. There are hardly any differences in grammar – especially at the level of educated speech. Those that do exist tend to be rather subtle. For example, the use of the modal auxiliaries 'shall' and 'should' with first person subjects (I and we) is rare in Australian. 'We should like to see you' is not common. It is more likely to be formed as 'we would like to see you'. In a similar way 'shall' becomes 'will'. This pattern is increasingly followed in British English.

It is at the colloquial level that the real differences emerge, especially with different usage.

Activity 23

'Can I have cup of tea, thanks?'

1 How does the construction differ from the Standard British English?

2 Think of any reasons why Australian English may prefer this construction.

Independent research

Many of the phonological differences are quite complicated, and will not be discussed here, but can be explored in Trudgill and Hannah's *International English* and David Crystal's *Encyclopedia of the English Language*, page 351.

Take it further

Using an appropriate linguistic source, research the meaning in Standard British English of the modal verbs 'will'/'would' and 'shall'/'should'. Are any important distinctions being lost if these differences are no longer observed?

Vocabulary

Again, the differences are relatively minor (especially when compared to American English) but much larger at the level of colloquial use. In fact, Australia is quite famous for the number of vivid idioms it has spawned such as 'scarce as rocking-horse manure' and 'bald as a coot', and their routine use of 'bloody' and 'bastard'. 'Where the bloody hell are you?' spawned complaints in this country when used as a slogan by the Australian tourist board (see the video at www.youtube.com/watch?v=rn0lwGk4u9o).

The more common occurrence of vivid idioms at all levels in Australian English marks its pragmatics as differing from British English (and American English) and shows the Australian love of informality. In Australia, it is far more common for first names to be used regardless of age, gender or status (compared to the American fondness, in the media at least, for 'sir' and 'm'am'). This does not necessarily signal equal status but rather the social value that Australians attach to informality. In what they perceive to be the appropriate setting titles and surnames will be used, but such settings are more restricted than in other varieties.

Activity 24

1 Construct your own list of Australian English lexical items and make a note of their corresponding British English terms. This is a good excuse to watch some Australian TV programmes such as *Neighbours*.

2 Are the words you have selected likely to cause difficulty if used outside Australian English or can they cross varieties? Think of any reasons why British English users tend not to use Australian English vocabulary (you may like to think of some of the issues you explored in AS Unit 1 Presenting Self).

In a similar way to America, the language of the indigenous people has also had an influence in Australia. The majority of Aborigine words are used to refer to the flora and fauna, and place names such as Wagga Wagga and Wollongong. Aborigine speakers have developed their own form of English. Explore some of the features and see how the pragmatics of their form of English differs because of their culture in Andy Kirkpatrick's *World Englishes*.

Activity 25

1 Think of at least three words referring to things that came to Australian English from the aboriginal languages. You may like to focus on the names of plants, animals or items specifically associated with Australia.

2 Why do words from the semantic field of flora and fauna in international varieties often come from indigenous languages?

Activity 26

Nearly everyone has heard of 'Waltzing Matilda' – if you didn't sing it at school you may have heard it at an Australian sporting event. Few actually understand what it's about – is he really waltzing and just who is Matilda? Below is one version of the tale without the chorus.

1 Identify any lexis you don't understand or which seems to have a non-British English reference. Is there any evidence of the influence of aboriginal languages?

2 What do you think these words mean? Use the context to help you with meaning.

3 Some words in the text, such as 'squatter', are used slightly differently from Standard British English. Try to identify their Australian English reference. You may need to search the Internet for some of the meanings.

4 Identify the meaning of the phrase 'Waltzing Matilda'. It has nothing to do with a woman called Matilda.

Once a jolly swagman camped by a billabong,
Under the shade of a coolibah tree,
And he sang as he watched and waited 'til his billy boiled
'Who'll come a-Waltzing Matilda, with me?'

5   Down came a jumbuck to drink at the billabong,
Up got the swagman and grabbed him with glee,
And he sang as he stowed that jumbuck in his tucker bag,
'You'll come a-Waltzing Matilda, with me'.

Down came the squatter, mounted on his thoroughbred,
10 Up came the troopers, one, two, three,
'Who's that jolly jumbuck you've got in your tucker bag?'
'You'll come a-Waltzing Matilda, with me'.

Up got the swagman and jumped into the billabong,
'You'll never catch me alive', said he,
15 And his ghost may be heard as you pass by that billabong,
'Who'll come a-Waltzing Matilda, with me?'

Writing in the exam

Please note the spelling of 'pidgin'. It has nothing to do with pigeons! If you spell it wrong, you will give your examiner/teacher a bit of a laugh but may also be marked down.

Key terms

- pidgin
- contact language
- simplification
- regularisation
- creolisation
- creole
- Jamaican Creole
- Jamaican English
- acrolect
- mesolect
- basilect
- patwa

Pidgins

A **pidgin** is a **contact language**. Pidgins evolve when people who don't have a common language have contact with each other over a significant period of time. In such cases people will draw on features from both languages to construct a new mixed language that can fulfil only limited communication needs. Both parties will still use their 'natural' language for 'home' use. Pidgins tend to be short-lived languages – they exist only for as long as they are needed – and they have reduced vocabularies and **simpler**, **regularised** grammatical structures.

Interestingly, the two processes of simplification and regularisation are at work in English dialects. Standard English has lost some grammatically redundant features, as you saw when studying language over time (see page 9), for example, we no longer inflect verbs for the second person) and there has been a reduction of the number of irregular verbs.

Creoles: Jamaican Creole

A pidgin language can become the most important language in a community, in which case it will be passed on to children and will fulfil a large range of social functions. If this happens, the pidgin will have altered and expanded considerably and is said to have undergone the process of **creolisation**. African American Vernacular English may have its origins in a **creole** via the slave trade. English itself may have originated as a creole via the Germanic languages, the Scandinavian languages of the Viking period or even from Latin. We can find English-based creoles in Papua New Guinea, West Africa and the Solomon Islands.

The better known creoles are found in the Atlantic, along the routes of the slave trade, and include the West Indies and parts of South America. Here we focus on Jamaican Creole.

Jamaican Creole is not to be confused with **Jamaican English**. Jamaican English is a variety of English in a similar vein to American English and Australian English.

In areas such as the Caribbean, several different 'levels' of language may be identified:

- **acrolects**, which are closest to the standard, in this case Standard English

- **mesolects**; in the middle, these versions are further from the Standard both grammatically and lexically, and show some features of creole

- **basilects**, which are far from the Standard, are deep creoles and difficult for British English uses to understand.

Jamaican Creole is often dismissively referred to as patois or **patwa**, which has negative connotations. Patois refers to forms of native or local speech, but the term carries notions of low-status users and language. Historically, the low social status of the users of such languages – plantation workers, slaves or simply just non-Europeans – was enough for early academics to give these languages low status.

There are a number of distinctive features to be found in the mesolectal varieties of English found in the Caribbean. The number and exact form of variation will depend on several factors – just like accent and dialect variation within the British Isles.

Vocabulary

Like any form of English, be it a regional dialect in the British Isles or an international variety, there will be a large number of words that are specific to that variety. It may be that these are words that reflect the Caribbean or adaptations of existing English words. You have already encountered this pattern in American and Australia English. Here are some examples of Jamaican lexis:

Jamaican English	British English
to carry	to take or transport
dread	terrible/excellent
duppy	ghost
licks	a beating
vex	angry

Grammar

Although the grammar expands when a language becomes a creole, there are still many distinctive features found in Jamaican Creole. Among the most common are:

- absence of plurality markers on nouns if other contexts make it clear
- absence of possessive markers on nouns
- absence of third person -s on verbs
- absence of the **copula verb** (to be)
- tense markers may be missing on verbs; instead auxiliaries or adverbs will be used
- in 'wh-' questions, the subject and verb may be inverted.

Several of these features are found in the regional dialects of the British Isles, indicating that there seem to be some areas of English more susceptible to change than others.

You may have already seen that English lost some of its pronouns over time – most notably 'ye' and 'thee'/'thou'. It would seem that creole languages have taken this process further. Regional dialects in the UK can also show similar patterns in pronoun use.

Key term

- **copula verb**

Activity 27

Read the transcript below, by Peter Patrick of the University of Essex, in which D recounts some of the violence surrounding Jamaica's 1980 elections. Much of phonetic spelling of the original transcription has been standardised here to aid reading.

1 Identify differences between the Jamaican Creole in the transcript and Standard British English.

2 Classify these differences into key constituents of language.

3 Offer explanations for why these differences occur.

> yes an' me tell you, you see, man … you have a guy up dere so
> him sit upon da ice box widout no foot, 's so im get shat up
> dem shat 'im an … mash up di whole a 'im foot
> so 'im only an wan foot now, an di piece cut off
> 5 so if you out upon di ruod an dat car drivin
> an a man jus' a-fire shat, im no business who it catch
> cos 'im inside a di car, an' dem no know
> we might fire back too an' catch 'im but dem a bad man.
> 's so = *That's how*

(Visit http://privatewww.essex.ac.uk/~patrickp/JCtexts.html

to read the full transcript and commentary.)

Independent research

Look at Peter Patrick's creole homepage at http://privatewww. essex.ac.uk/~patrickp/ JCtexts.html to explore a variety of transcribed examples, including a full transcript of the extract and a commentary on several of its distinctive features.

Independent research

Read Mark Sebba's article on creoles in Britain at http:// www.ling.lancs.ac.uk/ staff/mark/resource/ keynote.htm.

Take it further

This extract is from an oral story which has been written down. What evidence can you find to support this? In what ways does an oral narrative differ from a written one?

Writing in the exam

As well as discussing the obvious key constituents, don't forget that areas like pragmatics and discourse may be relevant. Remember that the key constituents you identify must be related to the context of the piece. In this case, context refers to the text's status as both an oral story and a creole form.

Phonology

Jamaican Creole has many distinctive phonological features.

Activity 28

The following extract is from the Jamaican folk tale 'Three Brothers and the Life Tree'. The story was transcribed from an oral tale in 1919. Its writer did not intend it to be a phonetic transcription but it gives a flavour of the original language forms.

> A woman got t'ree son. One day he said, 'Mamma, I gwine out to seek fe' a little work.' She said 'Yes, me chile, but care me little last son!' De mudder bake two pone an' after dey travel, de little bredder said, 'Bredder, I hungry!' He said, 'Dey only way you will get dis pone, let I pluck out one of yo' eye.'
> 5 De little boy said, 'Pluck it out now,' an' he did so. After dey walk a far way again, de little bredder cry out, 'Bredder, I hungry!' He said, 'De only way you will taste de odder piece, let I pluck out de odder eye.' De little boy said, 'What mus' I do after I hungry?' An' him pluck out de odder eye an' gi' him de balance of pone lef'. An' de two bredder walk, lef' dat poor one.

1 The phonemes /t/ and /θ/ are not distinguished in Jamaican Creole. Find an additional pair of phonemes in the text that are not distinguished.

2 Find any evidence of deleted consonant clusters in the text.

3 Using the IPA, compare the pronunciation of 'gwaine' (going) to the RP pronunciation.

4 What phonological process has the preposition 'fe' (for) undergone?

5 What phonological process, common to many forms of English, is indicated by the loss of the final letter on 'and'?

6 Pidgin languages tend to undergo much regularisation, but when they become creoles some of this may be reversed. What evidence, if any, is there in the text of the reappearance of irregular forms?

In the 1950s there was a great deal of immigration from the Caribbean countries to the British Isles. These speakers used and passed on their creole form and are now starting to influence some British dialects – especially in large urban centres.

English as a second language: Indian English

American English, Australian English and Jamaican Creole are considered to be first languages of their respective countries, but English also has a status as a second language in many parts of the world. In such countries it plays an important role and this will be reflected by its use by important institutions. Typically, these are countries that were colonised by English-speaking countries. Over 50 countries fall into this category, although only **Indian English** (IndE) will be discussed here.

Indian English is the form spoken in the Indian sub-continent (and is sometimes known as South Asian English). Once you have understood the general principles and are able to describe variation, any other second language varieties you encounter can be approached in the same way. Indian English now has the largest number of English speakers in the world, estimated to be 350 million! The use of English is increasingly associated with social mobility and the vast majority of these speakers use it as a second language.

As you saw with pidgins and creoles, there is variation in the form of English. At the highest social level, we find forms closest to Standard English. However, the younger population are increasingly disinclined to speak British English, seeing it as a legacy from colonial times. Increasingly, Indian English is becoming **nativised** – it has adopted some of the local language patterns, most noticeably in its phonology intonation and some words and expressions.

A number of different forms of English are used throughout the Indian sub-continent. This is because of the large number of different dialects found in India and the highly stratified social system with its class divisions. These range from the most basic 'butler' English – almost a pidgin – to a form near to Standard English. This means that any coverage of Indian English, especially in a space as short as this will, necessarily, have generalisations.

Pronunciation

The pronunciation of Indian forms of English can vary considerably depending on both the region and the education/social class of the speaker. But for most Indian English users the biggest difference is in the **stress,** rhythm and intonation. British English is **stress timed**, which means that each stressed syllable occurs at approximately regular intervals. Indian English is **syllable timed** rather than stress timed. This means that each syllable (both stressed and unstressed) is perceived to take roughly the same amount of time. This can make it difficult for those used to a stress-timed variety to follow those who use a syllable-timed variety.

Grammar

There are several grammatical features of IndE that are much more accessible.

Activity 29

Variation can be found in noun number and the use of determiners.

> Litters should not be thrown on the street.
>
> He gathered woods for the fire.
>
> Everyone pick up a chalk.

1 Why doesn't British English put a plural 's' on the nouns in the first two examples? You might need to explore the concept of 'mass' noun here.

2 What structure would be added to the third example in British English. Why?

Again, like English in the past and American English, prepositions can vary.

Activity 30

For the following phrases describe the differences between the Indian English examples and British English.

discuss about	pay attention on

Some of Indian English's more distinctive uses are found around the formation of the progressive aspect.

Independent research

David Crystal talks about Indian English as part of a radio series called *Lingua Franca*. Read the transcript of his contribution at http://www.abc.net.au/rn/arts/ling/stories/2005/s1298284.htm.

Key terms

- **Indian English (IndE)**
- **nativised**
- **stress**
- **stress timed**
- **syllable timed**

Independent research

Using some of the texts already recommended in this section, such as those by Crystal and Trudgill, explore the Indian English phonological system.

Activity 31

1 How would British English realise the following sentences.

I am understanding it	She is knowing the answer.

2 Why doesn't Standard British English use progressive aspect on these verbs?

3 Is there any evidence in colloquial British English of 'state' verbs being used in progressive aspect? (Think burger advertisements!)

One of the more confusing aspects for the British English user is the Indian English use of 'yes'/'no'.

> A: The man didn't go into the shop?
> B: Yes

In Standard British English the response would be 'No'. The Indian English user is confirming the accuracy of the statement – yes, that is correct, he didn't go into the shop. The intended meaning here is difficult for the British English user to understand.

Vocabulary

Indian English vocabulary shows substantial borrowing from indigenous languages, just like the other varieties you have studied. There is also a habit of extending the meaning of British English words and retaining more archaic forms – a reflection of the influence of the days of the Empire. Some words are combinations of Indian and English.

> lakh – one hundred thousand
>
> wallah – one who carries out an occupation, for example 'bankwallah'
>
> sahib – sir, master
>
> dhobi – washerman
>
> backside – behind, in the back of (this gives rise to amusing, at least for British English users, signs like 'Entry from backside only')
>
> Eve-teasing – harassing women
>
> furlong – an eighth of a mile (limited to horseracing in British English)
>
> hotel – restaurant or café (not necessarily with lodgings)
>
> tiffin carrier – lunch box

An Indian English language newspaper, *The Central Chronicle*, mentions the 'frisking and checking of vehicles' in a report on security. 'Frisk' is certainly a synonym of 'search', but would not normally be applied to vehicles and would be considered colloquial here.

Independent research

If you wish to explore the grammatical and lexical features of Indian English further, a wide range of Indian newspapers can be accessed through www.indiapress.org/index.php/English/400x60. www.thestatesman.net/ is the website for the oldest Indian newspaper in English.

Activity 32

Look at the following examples taken from Kirkpatrick's *World Englishes*. Try to identify the meaning of the Indian English lexis from the context and make some comments on their formation.

a His face-cut is very impressive.

b I came here in a tempo.

c He speaks chaste Hindi.

d Fifty students have applied for a freeship this year.

Activity 33   Read the following extract from *The Central Chronicle*.

> Vehicular traffic was not plying on roads and industrial activity had come to a grinding halt in response to the bandh called by Shri Amarnath Yatra Sangarsh Samiti (SAYSS), spearheading the ongoing agitation. However, traffic on the national highway from Lakhanpur to Jawahar tunnel in the province was plying normally, the sources said.

1 Use the context to identify the Indian English meaning of 'plying'. Look up its meaning in an English dictionary. Would you be likely to encounter its use with this meaning in British English?

2 Work out the meaning of 'bandh' from its context.

3 Identify a lexical item that is now more associated with American English. What phrase in British English shows that this word was once a common part of British English?

4 Examine the grammar. Is it similar or different to that which you would expect to find in a British newspaper? Find any evidence of non-standard grammar. Think of some reasons to explain your findings.

Independent research

Read the final chapter in Bill Bryson's *Mother Tongue*. Do you think that English needs to be protected?

The future of English

So, where will English be in the future? Nobody really knows. Few could have predicted that the obscure European dialect that became Old English would become one of the most widely spoken languages in the history of the world (Mandarin Chinese has more speakers numerically, but does not have the geographic range or number of second speakers).

The biggest question is probably this – will English remain one generally cohesive language with only minor variation between users or will it collapse into mutually incomprehensible sub-languages? After all, that is what happened to Latin.

Many linguists have taken the 'disintegration' standpoint, believing that English will form more new languages. In the 1880s, it was widely held that Australian and American would become mutually unintelligible. Even Robert Birchfield, the editor of the *Oxford English Dictionary*, speaking in 1978, believed that this was inevitable. He was applying the notion of **diversification** – the longer the varieties are apart, the more independent linguistic change would occur.

But that was 1978. And the world changes. Communications media was nowhere near as developed in the late 1970s and it is contact that prevents independent linguistic change. The influence of the Internet, television and the film industry mean that it is highly unlikely that these different forms of English will become mutually unintelligible.

However, another fear raises its head and one which is perhaps more realistic. Will the influence of Hollywood and the need for clear communication with a world of others through the Internet, and so on, lead to the death of any form of regional variation? Certainly, the number of languages in the world is reducing and high levels of literacy lead to uniformity. You saw this process in language over time (see pages 9–29) – the introduction of printing had the effect of standardising the language and there has been a loss of regional dialect forms in recent years.

The third option, and possibly the most realistic, is **bidialectism**. This is effectively a middle ground between the two eventualities outlined above. We will maintain our local dialects, but will also use a new international variety when communicating with the world.

Only time will tell …

Key terms

- diversification
- bidialectism

3 Tackling Section A of the exam

There are two questions on Section A of the exam based on separate but linked pieces of data. The texts used may represent diversity and/or change over time and date from the very start of the Early Modern English period (c.1450) right up to the present day. They could cover any mode – spoken, written or electronic. In addition, the texts will be drawn from a wide variety of genres.

Question 1 (a)

This requires a relatively short response and is based on a single short piece of data. The data could illustrate language change, language diversity or both. The focus will be on exploring the differences between the given text and modern or standard language use through the exploration of a number of examples. You will need to use precise linguistic terminology to describe the characteristic key features of the text and relate them to the notion of language change or diversity.

Question 1 (b)

This requires a longer essay-style response and will be based on additional, longer pieces of data. Like 1 (a), these pieces of data will be drawn from a variety of different sources and will show language change and/or language diversity. The texts will be linked in some way, often by genre, enabling you to compare and contrast them, and will be longer than the data used for 1 (a). The examiner is looking for evidence that you can identify the key linguistic features that characterise the texts, comment on and explain why such features are present, and explore and explain them in relation to the context of the texts. In such cases, context refers to the mode, field, function and tenor of the data. Remember that some areas of context will be more relevant than others and in the exam you will have to select the concepts that are most significant.

Assessment objectives

Question 1 (a) is worth 10 marks. They are split equally between:

AO2 Demonstrate critical understanding of a range of concepts and issues related to the construction and analysis of meanings in spoken and written language, using knowledge of linguistic approaches **(5 marks)**, and

AO3 Analyse and evaluate the influence of contextual factors on the production and reception of spoken and written language, showing knowledge of the key constituents of language **(5 marks)**.

Question 1 (b) is worth 40 marks. These are divided as follows:

AO1 Select and apply a range of linguistic methods to communicate relevant knowledge using appropriate terminology and coherent, accurate written expression **(10 marks)**

AO2 (15 marks), and

AO3 (15 marks).

Activity 34

1 Read the sample Section A 1 (a) question below.

2 Study the guidance above in pairs, and identify how the sample response meets the criteria for AO2 and AO3.

3 On your own, look for two other examples of key constituents in the text and relate them to context in a similar way.

SECTION A: LANGUAGE DIVERSITY

1. The following text is an extract from the *Journal of George Fox*. Fox was the founder of the Society of Friends, or Quakers, and was imprisoned many times for his religious beliefs. During a period of imprisonment between 1673 and 1674, Fox dictated his Journal to a fellow prisoner.

TEXT 1:

... And when I was at Oram before in ye steeplehouse there came a professor & gave me a push in ye brest in ye steeplehouse & bid me get out ye Church: alack poore man saide I dost thou call ye steeplehouse ye Church: ye Church is ye people whome God has purchased with his blood: & not ye house.

... then we went away to Balby about a mile off: & the rude people layde waite & stoned us doune the lane
5 but blessed be ye Lorde wee did not receive much hurt: & then the next first day I went to Tickill & there ye freinds of yt side gathered together & there was a meetinge.

And I went out of the meeting to ye steeplehouse & ye preist & most of ye heads of ye parish was got uppe Into ye chancel & soe I went uppe to ym & when I began to speake they dell upon mee & ye Clarke uppe ith his bible as I was speaking & hit mee in ye face yt my face gusht out with bloode yt I bleade exceedingly
10 in ye steeplehouse & soe ye people cryed letts have him out of ye Church as they caled it: & when they had mee out they exceedingly beat mee through a house Into ye street stoneing & beating mee: & they got my hatt from mee which I never got agiane.

(a) Select **two** examples which represent different key constituents of language. Using these examples identify and analyse the differences between the English used in text A and current English.

(10 marks)

Suggested approach to question A 1 (a)

- You are asked to select two examples from the text which differ from modern English and represent different key constituents of language.

- You must then use these examples to identify and explain the differences between the type of language used in the text and the type of English that would be used today.

- When you have selected an example from one of the key constituents, you must explain and analyse it. This involves explaining what the feature is, why it is present in the particular text you are examining and placing it in context of language change and/or diversity.

The following example for 'ye', 'ym' and 'yt' will give you an idea of what the examiner is looking for.

> **The key constituents of language are:**
>
> lexis and semantics
> morphology
> grammar
> orthography
> phonology
> discourse/pragmatics.

Sample response for question A 1 (a)

This text uses 'y' to represent the modern Standard English 'th' in 'ye', 'ym' and 'yt' (the, them, that). The origin of this feature can be traced back to Old English. The Anglo-Saxons had letters not used today such as 'þ' (thorn). This letter represented the modern English 'th' and was pronounced the same. Over time, 'th' replaced thorn
5 but thorn was still used on occasion, although its form had changed over time until it looked more like a 'y' with a dot over it. When printing was introduced (1476), a letter 'y' was used instead as they only had access to a standard alphabet and it was used in abbreviated forms such a 'ye' (the), 'ym' (them) and 'yt' (that). This shows how the development of new technologies can influence the form of English – in
10 this case its orthography. At the time, people would have been aware of this meaning and pronunciation as /Þ/, but over time this was forgotten and modern readers tend to pronounce it /j/. By this period, its use was quite rare but as this text was dictated, the writer may have used this form to save time.

Activity 35

Read the sample Section A 1 (b) question below.

1 In pairs, use the guidance (p 45–46) to write up an analysis of text 3.

2 Make your own notes on text 2 and then write an analysis of it.

3 Discuss with your partner, the key linguistic features and relate them to context.

4 Then write a final paragraph to your essay.

1. **(b)** Texts 2 and 3 are both examples of people chronicling events.

Analyse and comment on what these texts show about how changing context can affect the presentation of diaries and journals.

(40 marks)

TEXT 2:

The following is an extract from *The Diaries of Kenneth Tynan*, published in 2001. Tynan was an influential and often controversial British theatre critic and writer.

7 March 1975

Am in Brompton Hospital for week of lung-function tests to see how my emphysema's progressing. (Answer: no deterioration, but of course no improvement either.) Sharing a national health ward with five other victims, I'm overwhelmed once again by the efficient courtesy of the doctor, the patient niceness of the (mainly Filipino, black or Irish) nurses … Atmosphere in the ward one of uneasy conviviality, each man
5   privately seeking evidence to support his necessary conviction that he is less mortally stricken than any of the others. But the camaraderie is genuine: being in this kind of ward is like being in an air shelter in the blitz.

I remember when I first guessed that I had emphysema. It was at a party at William Styron's on Martha's Vineyard in c.1967: the table was candle-lit and after dinner the male guests competed in blowing out the
10 candles without pursing their lips (i.e. just forming an open O). Jimmy Baldwin, Terry Southern, Johnny Marquand Jr., George Plimpton, Philip Rahv, Lillian Hellman among the company. Of the men, I alone couldn't perform the feat, even at a couple of inches' distance from the flame. 'Aha' said someone (was it George?) 'that means you have emphysema.' When I got back to London, I checked, and learned with a little shudder that he was right. The party was held just before the publication of Bill's Confessions of Nat Turner,
15 already guaranteed (the grapevine always knows in advance) to be huge best-seller. Although with the imminent growth of the New Left ideas and black militancy among the Manhattan intellectuals, it was soon to be written off as a WASP bourgeois travesty of black aspirations. However, it made Bill a heap of money (not that he was short of cash, since his wife Rose is rich: but the kudos was badly needed): and as Rose was soon to be saying with immense satisfaction: 'It's Bill's turn.' Rose used this expression whenever a member
20 of the Quality Lit. Set had a big financial hit. A year or so later, with In Cold Blood: 'It's Truman's turn.' Presumably in 1969, after Oh! Calcutta!, it was Ken's turn.

Characteristic dilemma arises over Patrick Lichfield's wedding tomorrow. It's a shatteringly posh affair, with 1400 guests from the Queen downwards, and only today do I discover that morning dress and toppers are being worn. Possessing neither I am faced with a choice between (a) turning up in an ordinary suit and being sneered
25 at in the right-wing press for pathetically cocking a 'snook' at the affair, and (b) renting the gear and being accused in the left-wing press of having sold out to the upper classes. So it looks as if I can't go at all, much to the chagrin of K.H. who has bought a brand new hat for the occasion.

TEXT 3:

The following text is an extract from the *Journals of the Louis and Clarke Expedition* of 1804–06. The expedition was sponsored by the government, and was one of the first overland expeditions to the Pacific coast of America and back. A journal was kept as a record of their discoveries. This extract was made by the expedition's leader, Meriwether Lewis. The spelling and punctuation has not been changed.

Lewis
Friday, 2 August 1805

The vally allong which we passed today, and through which the river winds it's meandering course is from 6 to 8 miles wide and consists of a beatifull level plain with but little timber and that confined to the verge of the river; the land is tolerably fertile, and is either black or a dark yellow loam, covered with grass from 9 inches to 2 feet high. the plain ascends gradually on either side of the river to the bases of two ranges of high mountains, which lye parallel to the river and prescribe the limits of the plains. the tops of these mountains

5 are yet covered partially with snow, while we in the valley are nearly suffocated with the intense heat of the midday sun; the nights are so cold that two blankets are not more than sufficient covering. soon after passing the river this morning Sergt. Gass lost my tommahawk in the thick brush and we were unable to find it, I regret the loss of this usefull implement, however accedents will happen in the best families, and I consoled myself with the recollection that it was not the only one we had with us. the bones of the buffaloe and their

10 excrement of an old date are to be met with in every part of this valley but we have long since lost all hope of meeting with that animal in these mountains. we met with great quantities of currants today, two species of which were red, others yellow, deep perple and black; also black gooseberries and serviceberries now ripe and in great perfection. we feasted sumptuously on our wild fruits, particularly the yellow currant and the deep perple serviceberries, which I found to be excellent. the serviceberry grows on a small bush and differs from

15 ours only in colour size and superior excellence of it's flavour. it is somewhat larger than ours. on our way we saw an abundance of deer Antelopes, of the former we killed 2. we also saw many tracks of the Elk and bear. no recent appearance of Indians. the Indians in this part of the country appear to construct their lodges with the willow boughs and brush; they are small of a conic figure and have a small aperture on one side through which they enter. we continue our rout up this valley on the Lard. side of the river untill sunset, at which time

20 we encamped on the Lard. bank of the river having traveled 24 miles. we had brought wih us a good stock of venison of which we eat a hearty supper. I feel myself perfectly recovered of my indisposition, and do not doubt being able to pursue my rout tomorrow with the same comfort I have done today.— we saw some very large beaver dams today in the bottoms of the river several of which wer five feet high and overflowed several acres of land; these dams are formed of willow brush mud and gravel and are so closely interwoven that they

25 resist the water perfectly. the base of this work is thick and rises nearly perpendicularly on the lower side while the upper side or that within the dam is gently sloped. the brush appear to be laid in no regular order yet acquires a strength by the irregularity with which they are placed by the beaver that it would puzzle the engenuity of man to give them.

Capt. Clark continued his rout early this morning. the rapidity of the current was such that his progress was
30 slow, in short it required the utmost exertion of the men to get on, nor could they resist this current by any other means than that of the cord and pole. in the course of the day they passed some villages of burrowing squirrels, saw a number of beaver dams and the inhabitants of them, many young ducks both of the Duckanmallard and the redheaded fishing duck, gees, several rattle snakes, black woodpeckers, and a large gang of Elk; they found the river much crouded with island both large and small and passed a small creek on Stard. side which we
35 called birth Creek. Capt. Clark discovers a tumor rising on the inner side of his ankle this evening which was painfull to him. they incamped in a level bottom on the Lard. side.

Suggested approach to question A 1 (b)

- In this answer you have to analyse and comment on two diary entries. One is from 19th-century America and one from 20th-century England. As well as being written in different places, the function of the two extracts differs. The Lewis and Clarke text was an official record with an intended audience. The Tynan extract is a personal diary, which has since been edited and published.

- Read the texts carefully – don't just rush into the analysis, as you may make mistakes. Annotation is very important to help plan your answer, provide examples and to ensure you don't forget any important points.

- Make brief notes on the context of each text – its field, manner, mode and function (bear in mind the date of the text and/or its origin – American English, British English, etc.).
- Highlight significant features of language which reflect the various contextual factors. You should use the key constituents to guide you but remember that not all of these will hold equal importance in all texts.
- When writing your response, divide your time equally between the texts.
- Support each point with specific evidence from the text, either as a quoted example or, in the case of longer illustrations, a line reference.
- Use appropriate linguistic terminology.
- Make clear points of comparison and links to context.
- Avoid making judgemental comments about language. This could include describing forms as 'wrong', using terms like 'misspelling' when analysing older forms of English or comparing English from other communities unfavourably with Standard British English.

Below is a selection of features, in note form, that the examiner would be looking for in Text C. Remember, contextual factors are important and must be taken into account.

Contextual features that could be of interest

- American English
- 1800s
- Diary/journal to record events at the end of each day (possibly updated throughout the day)
- Purpose is to provide a record of new things they encountered
- Not professional writers.

Features that can be linked to various contextual factors (this list is by no means exhaustive)

- Lexis and semantics
- Borrowings from other languages (e.g. 'Tomahawk')
- American English vocabulary (e.g. 'Creek')
- Adapting existing vocabulary for new concepts (e.g. 'Service berries')
- Combining words for concepts not in British English (e.g. 'rattle snake')
- Use of abbreviations (e.g. 'Sergt').

Orthography

For example, 'colour', 'perple', 'crouded'.

Grammar

- Detailed noun phrases (e.g. 'beautiful level plain')
- Relative clauses
- Adverbials (e.g. 'gradually')
- Passives (e.g. 'are to be met with')
- Pronoun use
- Tense and tense shifting
- Sentence type.

Discourse

The relationship between reader and writer, for example, use of pronouns.

Section B: Children's language development

This section of the book looks at the way children develop language. In this part of the course you will study two aspects of Children's language development – spoken and written. You will also explore theories and research relating to those areas.

You will also learn how you can use the skills you have developed in the earlier units you have studied and ways in which you can identify areas you might like to pursue in your own research.

The first part of this section (Part 1, Spoken language) looks at the ways in which children develop spoken language. The second part of the section (Part 2, Written language) looks at the development of written language skills, the ways in which children begin to understand and interpret this particular system of meaning.

As they learn to write, children begin to understand the different ways in which the two modes communicate. Quite early in the process of the development of writing, you can see differences between the forms children use in written language and the forms they use in speech. In each section, you are given examples of children's speech and writing, but if you have access to young children, your own observations will help you to understand the processes described more clearly and to develop your own theories about what is happening in these early stages of children's development.

Each part works independently of the other, but possible links between the ways these language skills are developed are identified for you to consider further.

This section on children's language development covers the learning required for Section B of the exam, which will consist of a data-based question on child language. The question will be divided into two parts. Part (a) will consist of short questions that will focus closely on aspects of the data and require precise, linguistic responses (10 marks). Part (b) will require a longer response about specific aspects of the data you have been given (40 marks).

1 Children's spoken language

How do young children learn to speak and understand language? They can't tell us themselves and none of us can remember how it happened. The only way to find answers to this question is to observe young children in action.

No two children are exactly alike, but research into child language development shows that children develop language skills in broadly similar ways. First words are often used to name treasured people, animals or toys, for example. Most children (not only from English-speaking backgrounds) can produce /m/, /b/ and /d/ sounds before they manage to pronounce the tricky 'th' sound in words like 'this'. This section will introduce some key theories from research into child spoken language development. Simply as a means of organising the material, the ideas are divided into two areas. But, of course, these overlap and it is difficult not to stray from one type of question into the other.

- **Theories about learning** – What do we know about the way people develop any skills? What processes are involved in learning language in particular?

- **Theories about language** – What *is* language essentially – a structured system of sounds and words, a means of communicating meanings and functions in interaction with others?

These are 'big' questions and ones that have been investigated over many years. As with all scientific enquiry, as soon as one team of researchers completes their experiments and draws conclusions from the evidence, another challenges their theories by offering new data or a different way of interpreting it.

Assessment objectives

AO1 marks are awarded for selecting and applying a range of linguistic methods to communicate relevant knowledge using appropriate terminology and coherent, accurate written expression (10 marks from a total of 50).

AO2 marks are awarded for demonstrating critical understanding of a range of concepts and issues related to the construction and analysis of meanings in spoken and written language, using knowledge of linguistic approaches (19 marks from a total of 50).

AO3 marks are awarded for analysing and evaluating the influence of contextual factors on the production and reception of spoken and written language, showing knowledge of the key constituents of language (21 marks from a total of 50).

Writing in the exam

You will always be rewarded for taking a tentative standpoint. If you decide to name a particular researcher, concept or theory, make sure you do not assume that this is the final word on the subject. For example Chomsky suggests that children's language learning cannot be a matter of imitation, because of Poverty of Stimulus: he claims that the language they hear is so chaotic. Yet this transcript shows the parent speaking very clearly and repeating quite short, simple phrases..

You do not need to – indeed you *cannot* – know everything about this area of linguistics. What you will need for success in your A-level English Language is an open-minded spirit of enquiry. This writer's curiosity was sparked by the language development of her two grandchildren, Spike and Louise, from the ages of 1 year and 3 years, to 3 and 5 years, respectively. Armed with as much knowledge of research as a busy teaching life allows, I hope to lead you along some intriguing paths of exploration.

Applying the theories to data from only two children has limitations, but the advantages are great: you no longer have to cope with an artificially 'dry' typewritten transcript, but can listen to the live voices and understand the full social context of the talk. **You can access audio recordings of Louise and Spike on www.edexcel.com/cld-mp3**.

In order to enrich the range of data, go to other textbooks for transcripts or – ideally – your own experience of young children talking. Either make notebook recordings of their language or use a digital voice recorder, even one on a mobile phone. This alternative evidence may lead you to challenge some of the ideas suggested.

You will need to use your AS study skills in reading basic transcripts of spoken language. You should also be able to read and write the accepted symbols for the phonemes of English (IPA) used to represent the child's pronunciation on paper.

The following conventions will be used for the basic transcripts in this section:

Convention	Key
T-Nanny:	children's grandmother, aka Technonanny
Dad:	children's father
Mum:	children's mother
<??>	indistinct words
[xxxxx]	Standard English interpretation of previous representation of pronunciation, e.g. tandi [candle]
(3)	length of pause in seconds
(.)	brief pause
…	omitted words
<laugh>	non-verbal sounds or actions, also called **paralinguistic features**
/dɪs/	IPA transcription of word
(Is it?)	brackets indicate some of the words spoken by adults
?	to indicate rising intonation for question
!	to indicate exclamatory intonation
NO	capitals, to indicate emphatic volume or stress

Theories of learning

This is an area of research where psychology and linguistics overlap, hence the term '**psycholinguistics**'. The questions concern the workings of the human brain in regard to language processes. Some of the research has more in common with medicine and anatomy. For example, research shows that in stroke victims who suffer a loss of language use there is damage to the dominant (usually the left) hemisphere of the brain. Other research leans towards investigating whether any animals can be said to have language, in the same sense as human language.

The fundamental question for this part of the A2 English Language course is: How does a child develop language?

Activity 36

This activity explores what type of activity learning is and whether it involves different processes and skills depending on the situation. How similar or different are these four learning situations?

- Children learning to speak (CSpeak)
- Students learning a foreign language (SFL)
- Children learning to write (CWrite)
- Children learning to ride a bicycle (CBike).

	CSpeak	SFL	CWrite	CBike
It is essential				
Everyone manages it in the end				
It needs a lot of practice				
It just happens naturally				
It needs a teacher				
It is too difficult for some people				

1 For each situation, consider the factors in the table below and add others of your own. Add a tick for yes, a cross for no or a question mark if you are not sure in each column.

2 In groups, discuss your results. Focus on areas of disagreement and situations where you placed a question mark. For example, do you think that writing and the ability to speak a foreign language are absolutely essential skills?

In Activity 36, you probably came to the conclusion that there is something unique about a child learning to speak – it is 'child's play', if we compare it with the struggles involved in studying a foreign language. This is why some people choose the term '**acquisition**' rather than 'learning' to refer to the processes of child language development. Before you decide which term best fits the child's language situation, consider what is involved in the process of 'learning' various sorts of skills or facts.

Activity 37

Which of the following processes do you use and for what types of situation? Try to add other ways of learning.

- Trial and error – pressing any button to see what happens; trying another button
- Drills – repeating the same things over and over again until it becomes a habit
- Carrot or stick – conditioning by rewards or punishments
- Mentoring – providing shining examples to imitate
- Theory – explaining general ideas to apply in practice.

The following activities introduce some important researchers and their theories of learning applied to child language – B.F. Skinner, Noam Chomsky, L. Vygotsky, Jerome Bruner. This list offers you the 'usual suspects' – names that you are likely to come across as you begin your studies of children's spoken language development. It is not an exhaustive list – for reasons of space – so you may decide to take some side paths into the ideas of Piaget, Lenneberg, or others as well. This survey of concepts and theories, inevitably, stops short of the most recent research findings, so bear in mind that child language development is an ongoing debate.

Key term
- paralinguistic features
- psycholinguistic theory
- acquisition

Independent research
Use the Internet to find out about Broca's area and Wernicke's area of the brain and about studies into the language use of primates.
Go to www.TED.com to hear Susan Savage-Rumbaugh's talk on her work encouraging chimpanzees to communicate using symbols for words.

Try to get involved in the debate yourself. You will notice how this section mirrors a common pattern of academic enquiry: as one research team comes up with a theory, another group immediately poses objections and a different explanation, or suggests a slightly different slant. You should use the data in the activities to explore the concepts and theories. Test them against the evidence in front of you. Is the theory convincing? Does the concept help to shed light on the child's language use?

Remember that the first part on theories of learning is followed by activities on theories of language, showing how other researchers approach children's spoken language development from slightly different angles. Here we pose the question: Is it useful to see language as a system of forms and structures, or to emphasise meaning-making and the functions of language in a social context?

The functional approach to children's language was first introduced by the linguist M.A.K. Halliday as he observed his son Nigel. Although this approach is mentioned towards the end of the section (see page 69), you will find it offers many fascinating insights that have subsequently been taken up by other contemporary researchers. So, don't fix any of your ideas 'in cement' before you have reached the end of the section.

Behaviourism

The psychologist B.F. Skinner is associated with **Behaviourism**, the key principle of which was to base all explanations on observable data, not on intuitions or abstract theories about what *might* be going on in the inner workings of the brain. In the case of the animals that Skinner's team worked with, researchers observed the *behaviour*, the actions made by pigeons or rats as they tried to learn, for example, how to get the food they needed. Their experiments suggested that **conditioning** plays an important role in establishing habits of behaviour: if the pigeon performs a particular action (pecking at the drawer) and it gains a favourable response (food appears), then that action is **reinforced** and the pigeon is more likely to **repeat** it; and viceversa: if hopping on one foot results in no food, the pigeon will not continue to repeat this action.

Skinner then applied this research into animal behaviour to child language learning. According to behaviourist theories, the child tries out all sorts of utterances (behaviour) and is conditioned to repeat certain patterns by positive reinforcement, such as verbal encouragement or rewarding physical reactions.

There is some convincing support for this. At the earliest stages of an infant's vocalisation, if others respond to any cooing or burbling sounds with warm attention, the baby appears to be encouraged to use sounds for interaction. Conversely, a child whose words are consistently ignored or who is told to 'Shut it!' is less likely to see language as an effective skill to be developed.

It is obvious that children use words that they have heard others use. They may even repeat whole phrases, and they tend to pick up similar intonation patterns and pronunciation from language they hear around them.

Take it further

What objections can you think of, if any, to this step – from animal to human behaviour – in the Behaviourists' argument? Consider the related arguments for and against the laboratory testing on animals in medical research.

Key terms

- behaviourism
- conditioning
- reinforcement
- repetition

Activity 38

Read the transcript overleaf and listen to the audio file *1. her got her rattle*.

1 Identify evidence for a behaviourist theory of learning, for example:

  a adult's model use of language

  b child's repetition or imitation of adult's utterance

  c adult's positive reinforcement of the child's utterance.

Spike (aged 2 years) is looking at a picture book about Zaza and her giraffe family with his Mum and Dad.

Spike: what dis [this]?

Mum: that's Zaza

Spike: what dis [this]?

Mum: that's a grandmum

5   Spike: di di da

Mum: what?

Spike: her did dot didi [got baby]

Mum: yes she's got the baby oh yes did you say where did her baby go
        <looking at the picture book and telling story> ... so they can go
10   to the hospital and have a baby ...

Spike: her got her rattle

Mum: I think that's for the baby

Spike: her got her rattle

Mum: that's her rattle?

15   Spike: no her got her rattle

Mum: oh she's got HER rattle?

Spike: no her got he [his] rattle

Dad: the baby?

Mum: that's a boy

20   Dad: that's a boy

Mum: she's got HIS rattle?

Spike: yeah

Mum: ah! who's that?

Spike: <??> baby her got her rattle (.) a daddy

25   Mum: that's the daddy that's right

Spike: dat mummy

Mum: yes that's the mummy (.) what did he bring for the mummy?

Spike: fauer [flowers]!

Mum: flowers yeah

Take it further

1 How can
   Behaviourism explain
   the development
   of politeness
   conventions (e.g.
   'Please', 'Thank you',
   'May I') and regional
   accents and dialects
   in spoken English?
2 Compile further
   examples of
   language habits that
   can be 'conditioned'
   by parents, teachers
   or peer groups.

Nativism

The linguist Noam Chomsky attacked Skinner's theories in 1959. He put forward the theory that the ability to use language is innate for all humans and used the term '**Language Acquisition Device**' (LAD) to refer to the 'hard-wiring' of the human brain. In other words, he objected to the Behaviourist theory based on the notion that the human brain is a 'blank slate' on which experiences can be imprinted.

Chomsky's notion of a LAD cannot be proved or disproved, for example by dissecting the brain, but his ideas about the creativity of a child's language use are illuminating. If we listen to children speaking, it becomes clear that they do not simply **imitate** language, but constantly create unique utterances. No adult ever spoke the words 'Her not gone', for example, uttered by Spike and actually referring to a boy, not a girl.

Key terms

- nativism

- Language
  Acquisition
  Device (LAD)

- imitation

- virtuous error

- Poverty of
  Stimulus

Writing in the exam

You may wish to refer to Chomsky's theory of a LAD or his concept of virtuous errors in your exam response. But remember that every theory is just that – a hypothesis suggested by one researcher, inevitably to be contested (if not overthrown) by another. Make sure you have also considered the competing ideas of researchers such as Bruner (see page 53).

One way of looking at such child language would be to regard it as 'wrong' – a mistake that needs to be corrected by some negative reinforcement. Yet, there is evidence to support the theory that a child's language is not affected by correction before it has reached that developmental stage.

Chomsky used the term **'virtuous error'** to refer to non-standard forms which have their own internal logic that actually displays a greater intelligence than the ability to repeat words and phrases like a parrot.

Common examples of virtuous errors are the child's formation of past tenses in verbs and of plurals in nouns. If a child says 'holded' rather than the standard irregular form 'held', this cannot be the result of imitation of a model. Similarly, the child's use of 'foots' or 'feets' following the standard formation of plurals. It is unlikely that they have ever heard these words, so how and why did the child produce them?

Although it sounds odd to talk about 'data' and 'hypothesis' in an infant's experience, Chomsky's explanation is that the child perceives regular patterns in the mass of sound data and forms a hypothesis about the form used for expressing ideas about the past. The child has worked out that you add the '–ed' morpheme to the base verb. Not in those words, of course, but what other theory could explain such unique language forms?

Another important part of Chomsky's attack on Skinner's Behaviourist theory of learning is what he calls the **Poverty of Stimulus**. A child is not exposed to carefully planned examples of language, delivered clearly in small, regular doses. Instead, there is a cacophony of sounds – various people talking at the same time, possibly fast or inaudible, with interruptions, incomplete utterances and so on. It would be hard for an older person to pick up a foreign language in a matter of years, if that was their only input. So, Chomsky argues, there must be an innate ability for language.

Independent research

Find out about the 'wugs' test, for example, on http://childes.psy.cmu.edu/ or www.wisc.edu/english/rfyoung. What do such tests reveal about a child's understanding of morphemes (prefixes and suffixes) in English?

Activity 39

Read the transcripts below of Louise (aged 3–4 years) in various interactions.

1 What evidence can you find of creativity in the child's language, that is, utterances that cannot be the result of imitation, as it is unlikely that any adult has ever produced this language?

2 Explain why each utterance is not simply a 'mistake', but a virtuous error.

3 What does each utterance show that the child has understood about either:

  a general principles of morphology (word formation)

  b grammar (structure of phrases and sentences)?

Transcript A:

<whispers re. 'surprise' etc.>

Spike: Didi!

Louise: bo! bo!

<general confusion, feigned excitement, etc.>

Louise: you didn't <??> we surprised you did you shock?

Transcript B:

Louise: I can open the door on by myself

T-Nanny: can you

Louise: yeah see

T-Nanny: you're very smart

Transcript C:

	Mum:	so what did you do with Didi she babysat you today huh
	Louise:	yeah um danced danced I danced
	Mum:	you danced?
	Louise:	yeah
5	Louise:	and I sellotaped with paper
	Mum:	yeah
	Louise:	to make stuff
	Louise:	and I cutted with a little bit sharp scissors
	Mum:	really
10	Louise:	yeah and they didn't hurt my finger
	Mum:	did she watch you like cut to make sure you were careful?
	Louise:	no

Independent research

Listen to the psycholinguist Steven Pinker talking about 'The Stuff of Talk' on the www.TED.com.

Interactional theories of learning

The arguments and theories about whether learning (or intelligence) is an inborn, natural quality or the product of a person's upbringing is sometimes referred to as the **Nature-Nurture debate**. Jerome Bruner was also interested in the role that a child's environment has on its language development, in particular, the child's interaction with significant others.

To highlight the connection with Chomsky's theory of a LAD, Bruner coined the acronym LASS to refer to a **Language Acquisition Support System**. He disagreed with Chomsky's assertion about the Poverty of Stimulus, from which it is difficult to take models to imitate. Researchers, such as Bruner, agree that there is an innate ability, but add the important point that this natural talent is assisted by carefully structured input from significant people in the child's environment. Some theories use the term **'motherese'** to refer to the particularly supportive way a mother adapts her speech in interaction with a child. In recent years, people prefer the non-gender-specific terms **'caregiver language'** or **'Child-Directed Speech'** (CDS) to refer to any influential person speaking to the young child.

This simple summary of Bruner's theories about features of caregiver language is available on many websites:

- simplified grammar and meaning
- shorter sentences – from eight words per sentence to four (for two-year-olds)
- restricted range of sentence patterns
- expansion and repetition of sentences
- slower speech
- use of special words and sounds (e.g. 'blanky' for 'blanket, 'poopy' for toilet training)
- high pitch
- large number of questions and utterances with high rising intonation, looking for feedback
- embedded in the here and now (e.g. focus on things and events in the child's immediate environment, rather than reference to past, future, imaginary or hypothetical situations).

Key terms

- nature-nurture debate

- Language Acquisition Support System (LASS)

- motherese

- caregiver language

- Child-Directed Speech (CDS)

Take it further

Read the original ideas in J. Bruner, *Child's Talk*. Expand the simplified account given here and provide fuller examples for each point.

Activity 40

Read the following transcript and listen to the audio file *2. spike colours*.

1 What evidence can you find of care-giver language, that is, the parent providing carefully structured input?

2 Try to use any of the categories suggested above to classify each example.

Independent research

Find out more about the concept of Child-Directed Speech in Peccei, *Child Language, A Resource Book for Students*, page 44. What three roles are suggested for Child-Directed Speech?

Spike is in his bedroom with his mother. His sister is in the room next door.

	Mum:	push <??> come on let's get our pyjamas on do you want me to read you a book?
	Spike:	no one more time
5	Mum:	one more time? one more time after we get our pyjamas on come on let's get our pyjamas on and then you can do it one more time before bed
	Spike:	no
	Mum:	Spike!

	Mum:	Daddy's gonna come home tomorrow and we are going to make
10		him a lovely dinner do you want chicken for dinner tomorrow with Yorkshire puddings and mashed potatoes?
	Spike:	no <??> <??>
	Mum:	chocolate?
	Spike:	colour
15	Mum:	colours?
	Spike:	orange
	Mum:	orange? yeah I got you a shirt with that colour
	Spike:	colour! colour colour
	Mum:	colours?
20	Spike:	blue!
	Mum:	blue? there's blue (3) you like colours?
	Spike:	<*laughs*>
	Mum:	come on
	Spike:	look
25	Mum:	wow
	Spike:	look yellow
	Mum:	yellow! wow
	Spike:	look green
	Mum:	green? wow
30	Spike:	there green
	Mum:	there's green yeah and light green you mean and dark green
	Spike:	look brown!
	Mum:	brown?
	Spike:	yeah brown
35	Mum:	I don't see brown what Winnie the Pooh brown?
	Spike:	yeah
	Mum:	oh there
	Spike:	yeah (2)
	Mum:	well I'm sure glad you like your new room like this (1) pretty lovely

There are many directions you can move in from these theories of learning. For example, some researchers suggest that there is a **'critical period'** for language learning – if you haven't managed it by a certain age, you never will. There certainly seems to be an optimum period for learning languages. If you compare young bilingual (or trilingual) children, they speak several languages with far more fluency and accuracy than teenagers or adults manage after years of painstaking study of foreign languages.

Cognitive theories of learning

Piaget was interested in a child's overall cognitive development – their understanding of concepts, such as size and volume – and suggested links with their development of language. For example, the passive form of verbs is not simply a complex language structure, but a concept that children understand at a later stage, the difference between, for example:

> **The red lorry is following the blue one.** and
>
> **The blue lorry is being followed by the red one.**

The psycholinguist L. Vygotsky followed on from Piaget's work, developing theories about the importance of the wider social environment on a child's cognitive and language development. He believed that other people play a significant role in advancing a child's understanding. This might be adults, but could equally be an older child. This theory is applied in classroom teaching, for example, where group work is often used nowadays in the belief that other children can play a part in teaching, as well as the teacher. Vygotsky uses the term **More Knowledgeable Other** (MKO) to refer to this concept.

Activity 41

Read the following transcript and listen to the audio recording **3. MKO plait crib counting**.

1 What evidence can you find to support the theory that a child's language develops:

a alongside understanding of concepts, for example, the concept of age in numbers of years
and its relation to physical size, power or status

b with the help of a More Knowledgeable Other – the contributions of an older sibling.

> **Spike and Louise have just been left alone in their grandmother's bed to go to sleep. They spend about 20 minutes playing. This is the opening of their interaction. Louise has her hair tied up in two bunches, not actually plaits. Each child has a treasured bedtime toy companion: the Bat (for Spike) and Freddy (for Louise).**
>
> | | | | | |
> |---|---|---|---|---|
> | Spike: | what is it | | Louise: | yeah |
> | Louise: | aah! | | Spike: | <??> |
> | Spike: | what is it | 10 | Louise: | I said it's a plait |
> | Louise: | it's my bunch | | Spike: | is it |
> | 5 Spike: | what is dis <this> | | Louise: | Spike! |
> | Louise: | I said it's a bunch | | Spike: | <??> |
> | Spike: | is it? | | Louise: | that's a these are plaits |
> | | | 15 | | these are plaits |

Key term

- critical period

- cognitive development

- passive form

- More Knowledgeable Other (MKO)

Independent research

- Read more about the case of Genie, for example on Wikipedia. This was an influential case of a young girl who had been so severely deprived of human interaction that she had no means of communication apart from grunts, when she was rescued at the age of eight. Researchers wanted to find out whether she was still capable of developing language or whether she had passed the 'critical period' for development.
- Read more about Lenneberg, who developed theories about stages of development in children's language learning.

	Spike:	sit down	30	Louise:	well you're gonna be three – ee
	Louise:	these are plaits		Spike:	be thirty one
	Spike:	sit down! sit down!		Louise:	you're already two and if you go two one (2) that means you're gonna be no number
20	Louise:	I can do whatever I want to (3)	35		
	Spike:	me in my crib?			
	Louise:	it's gone		Spike:	yeah one (1) one (1) one (1) one two
	Spike:	is it right dere [there] (1) yeah?		Louise:	I got the Bat and the Freddy
25	Louise:	but we're gonna send it away	40		
	Spike:	but me want to		Spike:	three (1) four (3) um six an seven (1) an nine (1) an nine an three (2) an two and three <??>
	Louise:	you're a big boy			
	Spike:	no little			

Theories of the nature of language

Do Activity 42, before reading any further. It asks you to consider the nature of language, so that you can compare your own ideas with more established theories.

Activity 42

1 If someone asked you to explain what language is, or what language is for, how would you reply?

2 Compare your ideas with others in the group.

3 Feed back any ideas that are common to each person's definition of language.

Definitions of language often have two components:

• a phrase or word referring to its structure or form

• a phrase or word suggesting its use as a means of human communication.

For the sake of simplicity, this section will explore these two ways of looking at language. These approaches are not mutually exclusive, but they do indicate a slightly different emphasis:

• the structural approach emphasises the study of forms, such as grammar and phonology. The linguist, de Saussure, famously advised people taking a structuralist study of language to 'forget meaning'!

• the functional approach is sometimes called the 'communicative' approach, as it emphasises the function of language to express meanings. This approach emphasises semantics and pragmatics.

Structural approach

The first activities will ask you to observe the forms of language a child produces, using the familiar concept from AS study of the key constituents of language. One aim of this type of research is to find common patterns that most children follow in their development. You will, of course, notice that there are exceptions to every 'rule'.

Key constituents of language

phonology	the sounds a child produces
morphology	the roots, suffixes and prefixes a child can combine to form words
lexis	the type of vocabulary a child uses and the meanings understood
grammar	the structures of phrases, clauses and sentences
discourse	structures larger than a sentence – types (genres) of spoken language

Always avoid taking a **deficit approach**, in which you compare a child's language unfavourably against a model of adult competency. Remember Chomsky's concept of virtuous errors and do not use terms such as 'wrong' or 'mistakes'. Remember to take an open-minded, descriptive approach, emphasising what the child can do and bearing in mind the impressive skills shown in acquiring a complex system with comparative ease and speed.

Stages of development

There is a common way of providing a simple, brief overview of Child Language Development and that is to outline the stages of development in this way:

- first stage – **babbling** sounds
- next stage – single words
- then – two-word combinations
- then – **telegraphic utterances**
- finally … – the child reaches the pinnacle of grown-up language

This sort of account can be an interesting summary, but you should treat this approach with great caution. The reasons for this will become apparent, as you work through the following activities.

In order to explore the processes at work as language develops, however, it is fascinating to start from the very earliest evidence of language. When an infant begins to produce sounds, initially there are simply **reflexive sounds** such as crying, burping and laughter. Then the child seems to play and experiment with certain sounds. This develops into **reduplicated babbling** – a series of repeated consonant-vowel sounds, for example 'ba ba ba ba'. (Apparently, this is where the word 'barbarian' comes from! The Greeks represented foreigners' babbling sounds as 'bar-bar-bar'.)

Around the age of one year, the child produces babbling with expressive sound and intonation. It is, however, very difficult to represent – in the alphabet or in IPA – the sounds that emerge from an infant's voice box.

In this particular 'stages' account of child language development, babbling moves on to the **one-word stage**. Parents often think they have heard their child's first word as something approximating to 'Mummy' or 'Daddy'. But this might be a matter of wishful thinking. In most languages, the sounds for these words are ones that a child can produce early on (see page 68 on phonology.) It is no coincidence that early **bilabial consonant** sounds (m, b, p, w) are the ones produced with the lips – a part of the anatomy also highly developed for sucking, the infants' method of feeding.

Key terms

- **structural approach**
- **deficit approach**
- **babbling**
- **telegraphic utterances**
- **reflexive sounds**
- **reduplicated babbling**
- **one-word stage**
- **bilabial consonant**

Writing in the exam

As you work through your A2 English Language course, you might consider which 'camp' you are drawn towards – structural or functional. In the exam, however, you should try to approach the data from more than one viewpoint. A structural approach will involve close analysis of the key constituents of language (hitting AO1), a functional approach will involve consideration of the wider social context for language use (hitting AO2) and both combine in AO3!

Writing in the exam

- Don't provide a summary of these stages, as no exam question will ask for this. The tasks are always based on data in the form of transcripts and the data provided in the exam will never attempt to represent the babbling stage, for example.
- You may see examples of one-word utterances, but do not assume that this is evidence that the child is 'at this stage'. All of us employ one-word utterances at points in our conversation. You will rarely have data in the exam where the child's spoken language is confined to one-word utterances – there would not be enough scope for you to display your understanding of the subject.

Key terms

- holophrase

Activity 43

1 What were your first words – according to your parents?

2 Compile a list of 10 words that you think might be in a child's very early vocabulary.

3 Compare your list with other students' lists.

a What word class do most of the words fall into?

b Why do you think this is?

Because early words are often nouns, we might assume that the child is labelling things in its immediate environment. But that word can appear to mean something more complex. The single word 'teddy' might signify 'Here is my teddy', 'Where is my teddy?' or 'I want my teddy. Give me my teddy.'

Linguists use the term **holophrase** (from the Greek word '**holos**', meaning whole) to refer to the phase in Child Language Development when the child's output is restricted to one word at a time. However, these utterances seem to be capable of conveying as much meaning as a complete sentence. Certainly, adults interpret many single word utterances as fully functional language.

Exploring these potential meanings takes us into the area of functional linguistics – asking not 'What did s/he say?' but 'Why did s/he say that? What did s/he mean?' You will find it difficult to isolate one approach from the other, even though this book organises them into separate sections – structural approach here and functional approach on pages 69–72.

Activity 44

Read the transcripts below and listen to the audio files *5. Holophrase A; 6. Holophrase B; 7. Holophrase C; 8. Holophrase D*. The transcripts only record the child's utterances and can only represent them in an approximate form. You might try your skills in using IPA symbols for a more accurate transcription.

1 Notice the context in which Spike (age 1) utters the single words and their intonation.

2 Comment on how you interpret their function or meaning as holophrases.

Transcript A: 'da-dee'
Spike and his mother are at the meal table.
da
da
dadee

Transcript B: 'da-dee'
Spike and the whole family are at the meal table.
dadee
dadee
da
odadee

Transcript C: 'mamee'
Spike and his mother and sister are at the meal table.
mama
mama
mamee
mameeeee
mameee
mamee

Staying within the 'stages' approach to analysing child language development, the child begins to combine single words into two-word utterances.

Researchers have examined the early two-word speech of children and suggested that the structure could be described as a **pivot-open grammar.** The rules of this theory of grammar were quite simple, based on two classes of words:

- **pivot word class** – few in number, but occurring often in a child's speech
- **open word class** – a greater number, but occurring less frequently.

Using this theory of structure, an example of pivot words in Spike's speech would be 'more' and 'my'. He combines these useful words to lay claims to all sorts of things: 'my drink', 'more cheese', 'more telly', etc.

Activity 45

Read the following transcripts and listen to the audio files **9. Pivot A; 10. Pivot B; 11. Pivot C**. The transcripts show only the child's utterances.
You will notice that the person transcribing cannot be sure what counts as a word. Do you think that 'dunnit' is one word? Is 'open it' two separate words?

1 Try to analyse the two-word utterances in terms of pivot and open terms.

2 Evaluate the usefulness of these concepts in analysing the child's utterances.

Transcript A: pivot, more, my, mine

Context: Spike (age 1) and his mother

one more	one more	
dat mine	dat mine	dat mine
mine	my blanket	my blanket

Transcript B: pivot, open it, hug, mummy

open it	open it
you open it	
hug hug	hug mummy

Transcript C: pivot - 3 word

hey mine	yeah drink coffee
I dunnit	
dunnit mummy	
drink allit	drink allit

As you work through this section, you should be alert to the tentative nature of theories – they are just that and not statements of fact. Although some linguists and researchers suggested the concept of pivot grammar, others challenged their theories on the basis that the concept did not work well enough to explain the data. Using the concept of 'stages', the next stage is that of telegraphic speech/utterances.

The linguist Chomsky used the distinction between **surface forms (performance)** and the underlying **deep structure (competence)**, which is similar to de Saussure's distinction between **'langue'** and **'parole'**. For example, the same surface form 'open it' might have different interpretations of its function, depending on the context. So, it could mean on one occasion 'Look I opened it' (the deep structure of a declarative). On another occasion, it could mean 'Open it for me' (the deep structure of an imperative).

Key terms

- **pivot-open grammar**

- **pivot word class**

- **open word class**

- **surface forms (performance)**

- **deep structure (competence)**

- **langue**

- **parole**

Writing in the exam

It is relatively straightforward to identify the 'missing' words. In the exam, you will always need to take this identification a step (or two) further, by analysing and commenting. Always look for trends – patterns emerging from the data. Ask yourself questions such as Why? or Where else does such language use occur?

Telegraphic utterances are a condensed form of sentence structure without function words (auxiliary verbs, pronouns, prepositions, determiners). The term refers to the mode of communication by telegraph or telegram, where the sender had to pay per word used and so kept the message as short as possible.

> Arriving 10 am = I will be arriving at 10 am

Nowadays we might consider the analogy with SMS language structures, though it is important to keep some other factors in mind: such messages are often not 'stand-alone', but form part of an ongoing conversation.

> you coming tonite = are you coming tonight?

Headlines also use this method of keeping the message short:

> Motorway traffic chaos = The motorway traffic is in chaos.

Remember to avoid using a deficit approach as you compare the form of any utterance with an 'ideal' (i.e. which exists in a hypothetical realm), standard form of written grammar – the ability to write headlines, for example, is considered a skill. Similarly, you should investigate the telegraphic speech of children as evidence for their language ability. It tends to support the theory of an innate or inbuilt understanding of grammar. Children are clearly not imitating speech they have heard, but have an intuitive sense of the essential words (**lexical word classes**) for communicating meaning as opposed to the 'disposable' words (**grammatical word classes**).

Key terms

- lexical (content) word classes

- grammatical (function) word classes

Activity 46

1 Read the following transcript of Louise (aged 3–4). Identify examples of telegraphic utterances and analyse each structure.

a Expand each structure into full, standard grammatical sentences.

b Identify what classes of words are omitted.

c Suggest why these are not necessary to convey Louise's meaning.

> **Louise is chatting to her parents and grandmother over a period of time.**
>
> Louise: it like my movie
> Louise: it running out of batteries (Is it?)
> Louise: it working again I think now
> Louise: I got it now
> 5 Louise: now it your turn
> Louise: what is this? <*her grandmother explains about Tippex ...*>
> Louise: can I try it

Independent research

Find and analyse other examples of young children talking. Do they tend to omit all forms of the verb 'to be', saying, for example 'Me happy' or 'You having a drink'?

Often Louise omits the word 'is'. It doesn't take a language expert to notice that. When you begin to analyse, you consider what class of words 'is' comes into: it is a form of the auxiliary verb 'to be'. You could use the linguistic terminology for this particular verb, which is the most commonly used verb in the English language: it is called a copula verb (from the Latin, meaning to join or link), referring to one of its functions.

> I am happy. I = happy.

You should then consider whether children omit all forms of this verb, for example, 'am', 'are', 'were', etc.

Louise also omits the word 'have' (I got it now). Is there any connection? You might know that 'have/has' is another auxiliary verb, so Louise can communicate using only the main verb (got).

It is important to look for trends, but also important to be open to exceptions that prove (meaning *test* or *challenge*, not *support*) the rule. Did you notice that Louise did not omit the copula in the final example: 'What is this?' Can you explain this?

As you read transcripts and listen to other young children talking, identify any use of telegraphic utterances and analyse this feature using the concepts provided above.

After this brief look at child language through the 'lens' of developmental stages, it is time to try a slightly different approach. Using the same metaphor of placing the data under a microscope, we will now focus on each key constituent of language in turn.

Grammar

Certain aspects of grammar have been of particular interest for researchers into child language development. One area is: How do children manipulate structures to turn declarative statements into questions or negatives? Think about how this is done in English by transforming a few examples of declaratives. For example:

> She's going.   Is she going?   She isn't going.

Notice exactly what moves you have to make to change it into:

- an interrogative form – simply reverse the order of the subject and the *first* of two verbs
- a negative form – insert 'not' after the auxiliary verb.

That seems relatively straightforward as a manoeuvre, but then look at sentences in the simple present tense, rather than the continuous aspect:

> I want that.   Do you want that?   I don't want that.

This is more tricky:

- use of a completely new auxiliary verb 'do', instead of a simple reversal 'Want you that?'
- addition of a negative term 'don't, instead of 'I want not that.'

Across AS and A2

This section assumes knowledge from AS study of grammatical terms for types of sentences, types of verb and verb phrase, and types of pronouns. See pages 49–55 in the AS Student Book.

Activity 47

1 Transform a variety of declarative structures, using all the tenses, aspects (continuous and perfect) and modal auxiliaries. For example:

a	Simple past tense	They found it.
b	Future form	We will see.
c	Present perfect	He has finished.
d	Past perfect	He had finished.
e	Past continuous	We were playing.
f	Present perfect continuous	We have been playing
g	Modal auxiliary verbs	I can/must/might/should see it.

2 Explain each transformation as a move or series of moves.

Across AS and A2

This aspect of child spoken language development links with language change – these question and negative structures were used at some point in the development of English over time. There are also some links with language diversity (see pages 29–41 for examples).

You will see that the process is not the same for all types of declaratives, depending on the form of the verb phrase.

Children often develop question and negative structures in stages. They may start by using intonation alone to signal questions. Then they introduce question words: research suggests that 'what' and 'where' tend to occur before 'who', 'why', 'when'. You might reflect on whether this is connected to the language they have heard (Skinner imitation theory), their cognitive development (Piaget *et al.*) or even their particular communicative needs (Halliday's theory of language functions, see page 69).

Activity 48

Read the transcript below and listen to the audio files *12. Are you open it; 13. Her don't like em*.

1 List all the uses of question and negative forms by adults and children.

2 Analyse the child's formation of questions and negatives. For example:

Child's utterance	Standard written interrogative structure	Analysis
are you open it	will/can/did you open it	The child uses the auxiliary verb 'are'. This is normally used to form interrogatives in present continuous 'are you opening', but in this case it appears that the child is expressing a slightly different meaning, though we cannot be sure which is intended.

Spike is travelling with his mother, father, grandmother and sister in the car with an Easter egg gift.

Spike: it got egg in it

Mum: what did you say? it's got another egg inside of it?

Spike: yeah

5 T-Nanny: I think it's got chocolate buttons inside of it if you shake you can hear

Mum: chocolate buttons inside? Shake it! Shake it up and down! You hear those chocolate buttons?

Spike: are you open it?

Mum: you could just bite his head then you could pour some out of his
10 head

Spike: what head?

_____

Mum: I think daddy's going to want a button are you going to share a button with daddy?

Spike: no

15 Mum: <*gasp*> you're not gonna give daddy a button?

Louise: I am

Spike: but her don't like it

Mum: he does

Spike: no her don't

You may have noticed Spike's use of pronoun to refer to his father. Not only does he use the female pronoun, but in its object form 'her'. This is despite his mother contradicting and using the standard form 'he'. This, incidentally, supports the claim that motherese/caregiver language focuses on the truthfulness of a child's utterances, rather than their linguistic 'correctness'.

This chart of the standard pronoun forms in contemporary English demonstrates just how complex the system is:

	Subject form	Object form	Possessive	Possessive	Reflexive
First person singular	I	me	my	mine	myself
First person plural	we	us	our	ours	ourselves
Second person singular	you	you	your	yours	yourself
Second person plural	you	you	your	yours	yourselves
Third person singular: female	she	her	her	hers	herself
Third person singular: male	he	him	his	his	himself
Third person singular: neutral	it	it	its	its	itself
Third person plural	they	them	their	theirs	themselves

Activity 49

Read these transcripts of Louise (age 3) and listen to audio files *14. pronouns compilation*.

1 Identify the child's use of pronouns.

2 Comment on the forms Louise uses.

3 Add further examples from transcripts and recordings of other children.

> **Compilation from Louise speaking**
>
> I think me love her
>
> her thinks me love her
>
> her take it off
>
> him doing it
>
> don't eat HIS, eat YOURS
>
> me and my car it's actually your car
>
> No no not YOURS it's MIINE

Some of the more complex structures in language are the passive mood and complex sentences using conjunctions. Or, if you take a cognitive approach, these structures express concepts that are more difficult to grasp. Here are some examples:

Passive:	I think this idea <u>might have been assimilated</u> from experience of folk tales.
Active:	Someone <u>assimilated</u> this idea.

Complex:	You should let me have the book (<u>^that</u>) I bought, <u>as</u> it was a special present for my mother.
Simple:	Give me the book.
Compound:	I bought it <u>and</u> it's a present for my mum.

Even at much older ages, students are assessed for their ability to use these structures. In SATS and GCSE mark schemes, higher bands are awarded for the use of the passive voice in formal writing. Lower mark bands are awarded to students who rely heavily on coordinating conjunctions (e.g. and, but, or) to form compound structures.

Activity 50

Read the transcripts and listen to audio files **15. if they blow them up; 16. conjunctions**.

1 Identify the child's use of the passive voice. How do you think she developed this structure – by imitation or by understanding of the grammatical principle?

2 Identify the child's use of complex sentence structures.

   a Which conjunctions does she use?

   b Comment on any non-standard forms.

Transcript A:
Louise was chatting to her grandmother in the car, after dropping her mother at work one morning. They saw the famous Sheffield landmark – Tinsley cooling towers – that Louise's mother had used on a flyer alongside a bottle of Henderson's Relish, not beer as Louise thought.

	Louise:	my mummy has a picture of those
	T-Nanny:	yes I know, she took a very good picture of those
	Louise:	yeah and it has a bear [beer] on
5	T-Nanny:	and they're going to blow them up, get rid of them. They are going to explode them cos they don't want them any more
	Louise:	I do
	T-Nanny:	I know I do I think they're part of the scenery
	Louise:	If they knock them down the planet will be destroyed
10	T-Nanny:	do you think?
	Louise:	yeah my mummy told me that as a secret
	T-Nanny:	did she?
	Louise:	yeah
	Louise:	I know something what you've forgotten
15	T-Nanny:	what do you know?
	Louise:	you forgot something what I know still
	T-Nanny:	mmm?
	Louise:	some people are changing every road of Sheffield
	T-Nanny:	oh I know

Transcript B:
(Note: only Louise's (age 3) utterances are transcribed.)

ko why it clicked off

yeah ko why it won't work

I want it (What) that what you have in your hand

5 the special CBeebies book (which?) what I drawed in with my special CBeebies colour in pens

I found it there when you was asleep on the couch

Morphology

The 'Wugs' test (see page 52) demonstrates that a child has an understanding of the way words can be structured, adding prefixes or suffixes to a root word. It cannot be imitation, as the test uses invented words. In English, suffixes can be added to verbs to indicate different tenses:

jump jumping jumped

and to adjectives to express comparative and superlative meanings:

big bigger biggest

Prefixes can indicate concepts such as the negative. It is often the child's virtuous errors that demonstrate their underlying understanding of morphology. Louise, for example, was talking about a picture she wanted to show to her teacher.

Mum: I think Miss Allen will be impressed.

Louise: I hope she won't be unpressed.

Activity 51

Read the transcript below and listen to audio file *17. loud, louder, loudest*.

1 Identify the various suffixes used for the word 'loud' and related adjectives by:

   a Louise

   b her grandmother.

2 Comment on what Louise has understood about morphology.

Louise (3) is travelling in car with her grandmother back from a birthday party where she got some party whistles.

(Note: the key words have been underlined.)

Louise: do you know how to blow a whistle?

T-Nanny: yeah I think so

....

Louise: did you hear that?

T-Nanny: certainly did it was <u>very loud</u>

5 Louise: is that <u>pretty loud</u>?

T-Nanny: that is <u>pretty loud</u>

Louise: is that <u>quiet</u>?

T-Nanny: er yeah that was OK

Louise: I love <u>loud and loud and quiet</u>

10 T-Nanny: do you?

Louise: yeah do you?

T-Nanny: er <u>sometimes I like loud</u> but <u>usually I prefer quiet</u>

Louise: is it <u>funny</u>?

T-Nanny: ummmm ... <u>funny-ish</u>

....

15 Louise: I love blowing whistles

Louise: do you want to blow yours

Louise: it actually a trumpet

....

Louise: shall we have another one with only trumpet in?

T-Nanny: um yes as long as you don't play it <u>too loud</u> yeah

20 Louise: alright this gonna be (?) <u>very (?) loudest</u> that why it <u>funnier</u> that why it <u>loud</u> ko why it <u>funnier</u>

T-Nanny: mmm <*piercing noises*> it's good I like that

Louise: I can do it <u>really loud</u> like this did you hear it?

Independent research

Watch CBeebies to find out what sort of language a young child is exposed to on children's TV programmes. Is it similar to caretaker language? Is any type of interaction possible? You might also go to the CBeebies website to see how this develops a child's language skills.

	T-Nanny:	nearly
	Louise:	do you like that <u>loud</u>?
	T-Nanny:	well it was <u>shrill</u> <u>very high and loud</u>
	Louise:	um do you know what that means?
30	T-Nanny:	no
	Louise:	it means <u>nice</u>

....

	Louise:	is that <u>really quiet</u> or <u>loudest</u>?
	T-Nanny:	<u>very loud</u> <u>loudest</u>
	Louise:	is that it?
35	T-Nanny:	that was <u>quiet</u>
	Louise:	er you s'posed to pretend it was … er you s'posed to pretend it was <u>really</u> <u>LOUD</u> like this *<shrieks>*
	T-Nanny:	oh dear very <u>VERY loud</u> oh

....

| | Louise: | is that <u>loudest</u>? |
| 40 | T-Nanny: | yeah can we do something else now? |

Lexis and semantics

Although morphology focuses on word formation, it clearly impacts on meaning. This part explores a child's understanding of lexis and semantics – the relationships between words and meanings.

A child has to work out what a word means solely from the context of its use. No one can translate the word or provide a simple enough definition to help the child. This deduction from contextual clues can lead to some misunderstandings.

The term '**over-extension**' refers to a child using a single adult lexical item (e.g. 'daddy') to name all people who share the characteristic of maleness. The term '**under-extension**' is used when a child takes too narrow an understanding of a word's reference. A child might understand the word 'bear', for example, to refer only to their own toy animal.

Important semantic concepts are those that indicate relationships between words and other words. Theories of vocabulary learning suggest the importance of grouping words according to their meanings:

- **synonyms** express similar meanings (e.g. little, small, tiny, young)
- **antonyms** express opposing meanings (e.g. large, big, enormous, old)
- **hypernyms** express 'umbrella' meanings (e.g. family – mummy, daddy, sister, brother)

There are many directions for investigation into child language. You may be interested in researching the influence of television on children's language development. The popular media position is that television is harmful to a child's development and, incidentally, that the amount of television and video-watching is linked to social background.

At an early stage Spike seems to assume a system where there is just one word for each concept and one corresponding opposite. Spike agrees he is a 'little boy', but does not accept 'small' as a valid alternative. He has his own system of opposites: when asked if he was 'sick', he contradicted, explaining 'No, I happy'. This may be the same for other children, at the moment it is hypothesis.

Chomsky's theory of an innate ability for language is really restricted to the grammar of language. Once the child has acquired the ability to form sentences in a variety of structures (simple, compound, complex, declarative, interrogative, imperative), they still need to extend their vocabulary. How is this skill developed?

Key terms

- over-extension
- under-extension
- hypernyms
- synonym
- antonym

Across AS and A2

Remind yourself of the concepts of lexis and semantics, see the AS Student Book pages45–48.

Social environment debate

Research into the differences between one person's repertoire of vocabulary and another's suggests the vital importance of exposure to external stimulus. At an early stage, this can only be the talk that surrounds a child. This might include TV programmes, but there is debate here about whether television is a malign or benign influence. One important difference between TV language and live language is the absence of interaction from a television. In some people's opinion, television is the sound equivalent of 'wallpaper'.

Activity 52

Read the transcripts below and listen to audio files *18. ghost drink; 19. architecture; 20. fabulous*.

1 Identify interesting uses of vocabulary by Louise.

2 Comment on the influence of the talk in Louise's environment. Do you think she has 'picked up' these words from 'caretaker' adults?

Transcript A: Louise (4) is at the meal table with her grandmother and Spike.

T-Nanny:	Spike have you finished your <??>
Louise:	but I did finish all of it
T-Nanny:	really
Louise:	yeah
5 T-Nanny:	is that just a ghost drink (2) what's that
Louise:	it's a ghost drink
Spike:	<??>
Louise:	it's a ghost drink
T-Nanny:	right let's …

Transcript B: Louise (4) is in the car, her mother and grandmother are commenting on the new buildings they pass.

T-Nanny:	monstrosity of a new building hideous!
Louise:	that is ridiculous
T-Nanny:	is it? I don't like that either
Mum:	it's all very brutalist architecture

Transcript C: Louise (5) is with her mother, getting ready for bed.

Louise:	hey this <??> look in bed
Mum:	oh that would be lovely unbutton your shirt shirt and you're probably gonna need some sort of bottoms
Louise:	yeah but I was looking for the black sparkly pants to go with this to wear to bed
5 Mum:	black sparkly pants those aren't pyjamas?
Louise:	but I wanted those to go with the T shirt they look fabulous together
Mum:	they look fabulous together?
Louise:	yeah do you want to see …

Across AS and A2

You will need your knowledge of phonology from AS study to follow this next part. See AS Student Book pages 35–36.

Phonology

You have already noticed that very young infants can produce vowel sounds and some consonants, usually those made by using the lips. Child language research into the development of phonemes in English suggests some general points. Some are to do with the **place of articulation** (in the front or the back of the mouth); some to do with the **manner of articulation** (plosive or fricative).

Consonant sounds

Here are some generalisations about the emergence of consonant sounds in young children:

- **front consonants** (b, d, p, t) come before **back consonants** (g, k)
- **plosives** (b, d, g, k, p, t) come before **fricatives** (f, s, sh, v, z, etc.)
- plosives at the beginning of a word (book) come before those at the end (book)
- fricatives at the end of a word (Louise) come before those at the beginning (Spike)
- **consonant clusters** reduced to one consonant (granma = jamma)
- consonant clusters at the end of a word (orange) come before those at the beginning (green).

Activity 53

Key terms

- place of articulation
- manner of articulation
- front consonant
- back consonant
- plosive consonant
- fricative consonant
- consonant cluster
- eye dialect

Read the transcript below and listen to audio file *21. phonology compilation*.

1 Try to use IPA to represent the child's phonemes more accurately than the **'eye dialect'** – the use of the alphabet to represent pronunciation.

2 Use the evidence of the child's speech to refer to the theories above.

Spike is with his mother or grandmother (in different sections).

(Note: square brackets < > with a consonant inside indicate doubt whether the child produces the phoneme or not.)

	Spike:	me dive it mummy
	Mum:	you drive it brrm brmm
	Mum:	look what does she have
	Spike:	her dot her own tar
5	Mum:	she's got a car
	Spike:	yeah like mine
	Mum:	like yours nice one

	Spike:	loo<k> loo<k> mum
	Mum:	teddies <??> you're supposed to count how many teddy
10		bears there are
	Spike:	dirteen
	Mum:	no you start at one
	Spike:	one fee
	Mum:	you're supposed to start at one
15	Spike:	no me start at dirteen
	Spike:	thirteen sixteen one

| | Spike: | tan tastle |
| | T-Nanny: | sandcastle you're right |

Spike:	dot lello dot gee\<n> dot lello
25 T-Nanny:	you've got yellow OK

T-Nanny:	are those the tweenies
Spike:	yeah teenie\<s>

Although Spike pronounces /r/ with a marked **rhotic** (rolled sound as in Somerset varieties) after vowels (e.g. car), this sound often occurs late at the beginnings of words (the Jonathan 'Woss' type of lisp). Other late-developing consonant sounds (at average 4 years) are the fricatives at the beginnings of these words see table:

The most tricky consonant sounds are these phonemes:

• /θ/ (thin, thine) virtually unique to the English language
• /ʒ/ (leisure) which never occurs at the beginning of English words, but is common in other languages such as French (je, Jean, Jacques).

Vowel sounds

Although vowel sounds do not present the same sort of problems in articulation, there have been CLA research studies into children's development of vowel sounds. Here is one example. A study of 100 2-year-old children recorded the following:

	Fricatives	
Phoneme	Example word
ʃ	shoe
v	van
z	zoo
tʃ	change
dʒ	jump

Vowel type	Phoneme	Example
Short vowels	I	pit
	æ	pat
	ʊ	put
	ɒ	pot
Long vowels	Iː	peat
	ɑː	part
	ɔː	port
Dipthongs	ɑI	pie

You may also come across ideas about other characteristics of a child's emerging speech:

• unstressed syllables tend to be deleted, for example, 'a pen [pretend] story'
• addition of an extra vowel sound between consonants, for example, 'belu' [blue]
• assimilation of consonant sounds and reduplication, for example, 'goggi' [doggy]
• voiced/voiceless consonant substitution, for example, gup [cup].

Functional approach

The linguist M.A.K. Halliday developed a fascinating framework for analysing child language development, which emphasises the function of language as a communicative tool (rather than a system of structures). Some of his evidence came from observing his own son Nigel.

Halliday focused on human communicative goals – physical, emotional and social – even in very young infants in a pre-speech stage. He suggests four primary functions:

• **instrumental** – expressing needs for food, etc.
• **regulatory** – controlling the actions of others
• **interactional** – making sociable contact with others
• **personal** – expressing feelings.

These goals, Halliday suggests, motivate children to use language once they are able to vocalise.

Key terms

- **instrumental function**
- **regulatory function**
- **interactional function**
- **personal function**
- **heuristic function**
- **representational function**
- **imaginative function**
- **metalinguistics**

Activity 54

Work in groups or pairs.

1 Using only gestures or non-verbal sounds, find ways of communicating each of Halliday's primary functions.

2 Now express these functions using single words or telegraphic utterances.

At a later stage of development, Halliday suggests (fitting in with Piaget and Lenneberg's cognitive theories) the child needs to achieve further communicative goals. These help the child to interact with – and come to terms with – their environment:

- **heuristic** – asking for information
- **representational** – conveying information
- **imaginative** – telling stories, joking, even lying to create an imaginary world.

At an even later stage, Halliday suggests an informative function, which has no connection with the outside world. It is a sort of **metalinguistics** – language to talk about language. This is an important function of the language used in your course books, your English language lessons and in your own responses to activities and tasks in the exam.

This neat framework is based on the theory of one man. This does not mean that language has eight, and only eight, functions. Can you add some of own?

Activity 55

Read the transcript below and listen to audio files *22. functions*.

1 Comment on the functions for which the child is using language.

2 Try to analyse the child's language behaviour using one of Halliday's functions in each case.

	Louise:	done that one (.) shall I do this one now? The tambourine
	T-Nanny:	the tambourine I think would be very nice to do
	Louise:	then the pirate one
	T-Nanny:	if you like
5	Louise:	colour in the nose brightly pink
	T-Nanny:	mm-hmm
	Louise:	er do you want to draw in the little one
	T-Nanny:	no I don't want to draw I just want to have a rest
	Louise:	hey how about the telly
10	T-Nanny:	I put it on pause because we weren't watching it then
	Louise:	oh, I was
	T-Nanny:	what have you got eyes in the back of your head? How can you watch it when your looking this way and the television is that way?
15	Louise:	I can watch it with this like this see?
	T-Nanny:	but then you can't colour
	Louise:	I can like this um let me just colour see?
	T-Nanny:	well it was getting noisy and annoying

Discourse and pragmatics

The concepts of **discourse** and **pragmatics** often overlap. As you study the overall discourse structure and conventions of certain types of spoken language (phone conversations, anecdotes, stories, jokes, etc.), you may also be drawn into consideration of the underlying assumptions and implied meanings of certain types of language behaviour.

Genre conventions

If you think of all the spoken language exchanges you are involved in over a week, you will be able to add to the list above. Your social awareness of the appropriate language behaviour for each is so instinctive, that you may not be aware that there are conventions (almost 'rules') for each – until someone flouts them!

Children gradually acquire – or perhaps it is more accurate to say that they learn them by imitation and reinforcement – these discourse conventions. Louise used to open telephone conversations with a specific account of whatever was on her mind/in her field of vision at that moment. Now, aged five, she is aware that the conversation needs to begin with some social orientation, for example 'How are you? Fine, thanks.' She also uses some **discourse markers** (also know as a **framing move**, these words are often adverbs, e.g. right, OK, now) to signal a leap into a personal anecdote: 'Granma, do you know something?'

Another handy discourse marker is the word 'actually'. Louise has used it frequently for years and now Spike (aged 3) has just discovered its usefulness.

Fairy stories often follow set conventions for the beginning and end: 'Once upon a time … they all lived happily ever after.'

Across AS and A2

Remind yourself of the following terms and concepts from your AS studies.
- Discourse is the study of structures larger than a single sentence (e.g. whole text structure, genre conventions).
- Pragmatics is the study of language in use. Rather than focusing on the surface structure of an utterance – what the *sentence* means – pragmatics is interested in what the *speaker* means in this particular instance.

Activity 56

Read the transcripts below and listen to the audio file *23. knock knock*.

1 Comment on what the child has learned about the conventions of telling jokes and stories.

Louise (4) and her mother and grandmother

T-Nanny: knock knock
Louise: who's there?
T-Nanny: police
Louise: who?
5 T-Nanny: perlease stop telling me knock knock jokes
—————————
Louise: knock knock
Mum: who's there?
Louise: pee/pay – piss?
Mum: you shouldn't say piss that's very rude
—————————
10 Louise: knock knock
Mum: who's there?
Louise: poo poo
Mum: who?
—————————
Louise: knock knock
15 Mum: who's there
Louise: poop
Mum: poop who?
Louise: <??> a cow

Louise and her American cousin Lanna are playing alone together in the garden.

Louise: pretend you wasn't normal <??> long long time ago and you wasn't normal…
Lanna: <??>
5 Louise: you wasn't normal <??> big witch
Lanna: who are you?
Louise: I am another witch <??> another witch <??> nice again
10 Lanna: <??>
Louise: no you I told you <??> it wasn't <??> for ever <??> wasn't awake
Lanna: <??> wasn't today
15 Louise: <singing>
then we found the witches and made her all to dead her won't wake up for a thousand
20 years till it 60 years
Louise: ha ha ha <witchy voice>
<whispering witchy things>

Key terms

- discourse
- pragmatics
- discourse marker/ framing move
- hedging
- mitigated imperative

Politeness conventions

Children need to adjust to the apparent contradiction – in order to fulfil your own selfish desires, you have to fit in with other people's needs. The skills of social interaction are paramount. Call it diplomacy, or the simplest politeness conventions such as 'Please' and 'Thank you', but awareness of the particular needs of a range of social situations is an essential aspect of language skills.

There are several adverbs that are never included in English language textbooks, even though they are used often and very influential. They add little in the way of informative content, but they serve as great social softeners. The linguistic term is '**hedging**'. **Mitigated imperatives** alter the strength of a demand by adding one of these words: 'I just wanted to …', 'Actually I wanted …'. Another word can be added as a hedge: 'It's not going to be possible though'.

Other politeness strategies involve an initial agreement followed by a contradiction (e.g. Yeah but …) or the use of modal auxiliary verbs (e.g. Can I/ you?, Should I?). Phrasing a demand as a friendly suggestion is often effective, particularly in its informal pronunciation, as in 'how 'bout …?' The pleading word is always an option, often used in isolation with stress and a rising intonation: 'Please!'

Activity 57

Read the examples of Louise's use of politeness conventions below.

1 Comment on what the child has learned about language as social interaction.

2 What markers of politeness does the child use – hedges, mitigated imperatives (e.g. please, though, just, how 'bout, can I?, should I?, yeah but), or a few in combination for added effect!

Example A: modal requests

should I do …	should I colour in …	how 'bout …
can I use these	I can't open it though	yes you did
very difficult to open though can you open it please		just

Examples B: discourse functions

Trying to explain	can you just press this please
Relentless repetition	look look mum I want this one I want... I want a big plate and a knife can I have I just need some bread please
Louise and Spike negotiating at bedtime	yeah but... yeah but... can I just do one puzzle PLEASE spike - No yeah but... I just need can I just...one Spike - No
Arguing (about make up)	can I put no I mean ... just yeah but my mum says
Compilation	let me just go and check

2 Children's written language

This part of the book looks at children's writing: the way children learn to write, the features of their early writing and the processes that lead to competence in the world of written language.

Introduction

Learning to read and write is often seen as a process that is separate from children's acquisition of spoken language. Should this be the case? Do children learn how to read and write when they start school, or do they acquire the skills of literacy long before they enter the formal education system?

As you work through this unit, you might find it useful to refer back to some of the theories about the development of spoken language and consider how they might be applied to the ways in which children develop written language skills.

Activity 58

Make a list of all the writing you have done in the past 24 hours.

a What did you write?

b Why did you write?

Most writing is done for a purpose. We write to record things (e.g. diaries, lecture notes, memos, reminders), we write to communicate with someone who is not present (e.g. letters, notes, notices) and we write to express ourselves or to record the fact of our existence (e.g. creative writing, graffiti).

We don't write for the sake of writing, the same way we don't speak for the sake of speaking. Language is a medium of communication.

So why do young children write? They live in a world of language and signs, and they have a powerful capacity to discover. As you will know already, children acquire language – they are not taught how to speak and listen. Similarly, children experience written language, both reading and writing, long before they enter the education system and formal teaching starts.

Activity 59

1 Two-year-old Jo makes a scribble on a sheet of paper and then identifies it as a drawing when she says, 'Mummy'. What fundamental concept about language has she understood?

2 This picture is Lucy's drawing of her father.

  a What aspects of her father are important to her?

  b What does this picture tell you about the child's view of the human form?

Spoken and written language involve a child understanding an important concept about language – that the sounds people make or marks on paper can mean something, that *this* (a sound, a scribble, an image, a symbol) stands for *that* (some object or concept in the world).

Activity 60

Ceci n'est pas une pipe.

The painter René Magritte produced this painting. Beneath the image, he has written *Ceci n'est pas une pipe* (this is not a pipe). Why did Magritte write this, and why did he call his painting 'The treachery of images'?

Images belong to one of many systems for expressing the world. Language is another. Children will be exposed to all of these from birth. Children have a powerful facility to understand how systems of meaning work, and the world in which they grow up is filled with these systems, all of which they will have to sort out and learn to understand.

Language is a way of coding the world into signs. Babies are often held close to the human face and adults often position themselves so that their faces are close to young children when they talk to them. It isn't surprising that to a child, an adult's face is the most important part. Most children go through a period of drawing people as large heads with the arms and legs attached. This is how they encode the world they see into marks on paper.

When early childhood literacy first began to be studied at the beginning of the last century, it was believed that children could not gain any literacy skills on their own and that literacy was a skill that was taught in schools by teachers. The focus of research was reading and this concentrated on the link between sound (phoneme) and symbol (letter). It was believed that until they reached a certain age, children were not ready to read and there was little point in teaching them.

More recent research has expanded the definition of literacy to observe the different ways children make and interpret meaning, and the way this leads into the understanding of reading and writing.

Activity 61

Discuss in groups the reasons why children at the beginning of the last century, and in previous centuries, were unlikely to read without formal schooling.

A world of signs

The 21st-century urban child grows up in a rich textual landscape in which they will experience a vast range of texts in a multimodal environment. The world offers this child an environment rich with logos, billboards, graffiti, tags, street signs, texts on garments people are wearing, texts on buses and other vehicles, etc. There is also sound – music from a range of sources and a huge variety of language offering the full range of cultural and social diversity.

Activity 62

1 Make a list of as many examples you can think of in one minute of signs that you experience daily.

2 Group these signs into different types, for example, information signs, instruction signs, indoor signs, outdoor signs.

3 How do you understand what they mean?

Across AS and A2

You will have studied meaning in short texts in Unit 1. In some of these, graphology will have been an important aspect of the text. How widespread was the language of signs and logos 100 years ago? 200 years ago? How different are the logos in western cultures from logos in other cultures?

As your own list will demonstrate, the use of signs to convey meaning is integral to 21st-century life in a way that it wasn't in earlier times. We live in a world of signs. The means we use to communicate are far wider than those used in earlier centuries. We use, and young children are exposed to, a vast range of sign systems in our everyday life. These systems include the language we speak, read and write, the clothes we wear (think about the signals you send out when you choose to wear a particular garment), the traffic signals on our streets, the logos of the different organisations that operate within our culture, the numbers we use to count. All of these carry meaning we can understand and interpret.

These signs are part of a child's environment from the earliest days of its life. Inside the home, the child is exposed to signs in other ways: toys, clothes, TV, food, adult reading materials such as newspapers.

The structure of signs

A sign consists of two parts – meaning and form. Look at this road sign.

Its form consists of a red triangle, an image that represents a car and an image that represents sliding. The images don't resemble the thing they represent – they have picked out what our culture has at some stage agreed are the important aspects of cars and slippery roads. The meaning of the sign is a warning (signalled by the form 'red triangle') that the road ahead is slippery (signalled by the representation of a car skidding). When Lucy draws a picture of her father (see page 73), she also translates her experience into a sign.

Language is another system of signs: spoken language is formed from sounds that, when put together in certain ways, create meaning. Written language is formed from marks on a page that create meaning when combined in particular ways. In order to write, children have to absorb and understand this code.

Environmental print

Parents often report that children as young as 12 months will recognise the signs they see daily, for example the logo of the supermarket they visit regularly, and respond to them. Children may not give the same meaning to a sign that an adult will give. One mother said, 'I was pushing him along the road near my mum's when he saw the Tesco sign. He got really excited and started pointing and making an *uh uh uh* noise, because he gets sweets when we go shopping.' This child, at this age, had made the reasonable interpretation that the Tesco sign meant 'sweets'.

Signs can be made from many different materials. The **mode** depends on the social and cultural context in which the sign is used. The sign for the Co-op is made from the graphemes (letters) <c> <o> <o> <p> arranged in a square. They are underlined and the logo is blue on a white background. Other signs might contain no writing at all.

Children make signs constantly, from the sounds they make; the toys they play with; from paper, paste, pens, scissors, cardboard boxes, furniture. A chair with a blanket may be a tent, a ship, a car, a house. All the resources of a child's world are available and used to create meaning. It's hardly surprising that they bring this facility to all the signs, including written language, that they see in the world around them.

Independent research

If you have access to a pre-school child or children, show them some supermarket logos and observe how many they recognise and understand.

Key term
• mode

Later studies into children's literacy started taking children's early experience of signs into account. In 1982, two researchers in Buenos Aires, Emilia Ferreiro and Ana Teberosky, argued that children's early writing needed to be seen in the context of their experience of writing in everyday life:

> It is absurd to imagine that four – or five – year old children growing up in an urban environment that displays print everywhere (on toys, on billboards and road signs, on their clothes, on TV) do not develop any ideas about this cultural object until they find themselves sitting before a teacher.

Observing young children quickly demonstrates how much they experience written forms of language through:

- **environmental print**
- being read to by adults
- observing adults reading
- involving themselves in writing tasks (e.g. writing shopping lists, 'writing' their name on cards and notes)
- drawing
- using reading and writing in imaginative play.

What seems to matter to the child is that the activity is meaningful and relevant to them. Observing young children will demonstrate how much they understand about writing.

Key term

- environmental print

Activity 63

Bethany, aged 3 years 6 months, is beginning to recognise the letters of her name. Walking home from school with her friend Emma, she saw the sign 'BANK' and said 'Look, that's a B for Bethany'. Later on the walk, she saw the road sign 'ENDCLIFFE') and said 'Looks there's a B for Emma'. Later the same week she said, 'When I'm 4, I won't be B for Bethany any more, will I?' Shortly after this, she made a picture from coloured stickers. When she had finished, she chose a pen, made marks at the bottom of the picture and said: 'This says Bethany.'

What does Bethany understand about written language at this stage?

a Does she understand the writing is different from drawing?

b Does she understand how writing communicates (visually and phonologically)?

c What link is she making between letters and numbers?

Very young children, before the start of formal schooling, can make the distinction between pictures and writing. Bethany's writing of her name is very different from the sticker picture she created. There is a clear indication that she is aware that writing is different from drawing. It looks different and it is used for different purposes.

She also knows that letters stand for something. She hasn't quite grasped the concept of the phonetic link between letter and sound, but she can recognise the initial letter of her own name and that of her friend Emma. She is drawing on her experience not just of print, but all the systems of meaning she has experienced in her day-to-day world.

Modern children interact constantly with their environment and the use of signs to communicate is part of that environment from day one. They will start interpreting this medium of communication and using it long before they start formal schooling. They know that when they put their coat on, they are going out; they know that when they see plates and cutlery being set out, they are going to eat.

Gunther Kress believes that understanding the ways in which children create meaning is fundamental to understanding the way their literacy develops. He says, '(a) we cannot understand how children find their way into print unless we understand the principles of their meaning making. (b) Children make meaning in an absolute plethora of ways, with an absolute plethora of means, in two, three and four dimensions.'

How does written language fit into this broad development of the understanding of signs? In earlier centuries, children were not routinely exposed to all the forms of environmental literacy that they are today. Advertising and logos are largely products of the 20th and 21st centuries. Books were expensive and not accessible to most people. The massive range of children's books that we see today did not exist. If children are not exposed to a specific system, it is unlikely they will develop the use of it.

Early literacy

Lev Vygotsky, working in the 1930s, proposed that 'make-believe play, drawing, and writing can be viewed as different moments in an essentially unified process of development of written language'.

When he was researching children's cognitive skills, he put forward the theory of the zone of proximal development: 'the distance between the actual developmental level as determined by independent problem solving and the level of potential development as determined through problem solving under adult guidance, or in collaboration with more capable peers'. In other words, children who seem to lack certain skills when tested on their own may perform more effectively in the social context provided by someone with the necessary knowledge.

For example, when Josie is reading a book with her mother (see Activity 67, page 81), she shows a clearer understanding of the text than when she is reading it on her own. Another example can be seen in the texts for Activity 73 (see page 88), where the teacher has modelled the form 'train ride' for the children to copy.

Skills the child shows in the situation where they are being supported by a more experienced person (adult or older child), but not when they are working on their own fall within the zone of proximal development.

Early research into childhood literacy failed to take into account all the ways very young children engaged with signs and interpreted (and communicated) the world around them. Even now, formal schooling tends to focus on one set of signs, those of reading and writing. Others tend to be downplayed or ignored.

Across AS and A2

Exploring the ways that writing for young children has changed in the light of developments in literacy would be an interesting topic for an English Language investigation (see Unit 4, pages 98–103).

Independent research

Books for children in previous centuries tended to be educational texts, texts written for religious and moral instruction. Read C.M. Hewins's article about the history of children's books on www.theatlantic. com/doc/188801/ childrens-books to find out when books were first written for young children and how the form and function of these has changed over the centuries.

Take it further

Can Vygotsky's theories about children's cognitive development be applied to written as well as spoken language?

Activity 64

In groups, discuss your earliest memories of reading and writing.

- Where were you reading?
- Who was reading to you?
- What was being read?

- What were you writing?
- Where were you writing it?
- Why were you writing?

Key terms

- emergent literacy
- emergent reading
- emergent writing

Are your early memories of reading and writing positive or negative? Research suggests that early experience of written text can influence the later development of literacy skills.

This first stage of literacy has been called **emergent literacy**. The term is used by theorists and researchers in the field to describe the early stages of the development of literacy, the stages when children perform reading- or writing-like behaviour. There is no agreed definition of this term, though Alonzo B. Anderson, William H. Teale and Elette Estrada, researchers in the field, have offered the following:

- **Emergent literacy** – Any reading or writing-like behaviour which mimics components of the activities that are generally considered reading and writing. There is no agreed moment when reading and writing may be said to begin. The school system often assumes that children know nothing about literacy and must be taught from scratch.

- **Emergent reading** – Any occasion upon which an individual comprehends (or attempts to comprehend) a message encoded in graphic signs.

- **Emergent writing** – Any occasion upon which an individual mechanically manipulates appropriate tools to produce (or attempt to produce) graphic signs representing oral speech.

As you will have observed earlier, children experience language from the moment they are born, or even earlier, some theorists would argue. As their speech and language develop, they acquire skills that are important in the development of literacy. They communicate though a range of media. They play, they draw, they construct models. They 'read' signs that are meaningful in their lives. They express and interpret meanings in mark-making and drawing as well as in speaking and writing. At some stage in their development, they recognise that speech can be written down.

Sammy, aged 3 years 1 month, sees the packet containing her favourite breakfast cereal on the supermarket shelf. She says, 'Porridge!' (She over-generalises 'porridge' to all breakfast cereals). Later she writes a shopping list as she is waiting to go out with her mother. She makes a series of marks on the paper, points at them and says, 'That says porridge'.

Children understand that language has meaning, and this includes written language. The drive to interpret meaning underlies the development of literacy.

Literacy practices in the home

Studies of literacy in the home environment have demonstrated the importance of this early experience, and the importance of taking it into account when children first enter the school system. William Labov's study of children's spoken language, *The Logic of Non-Standard English*, demonstrates how children's skills can be dismissed by well-meaning educationalists who do not understand a child's background and culture.

In 1983, Shirley Brice Heath studied the language and literacy practices of two small town communities in America – one black and working class (Trackton), one while and working class (Roadville). She also looked at the practices in an urban, middle-class community, which produced the majority of teachers in the community schools. Heath noted that the literacy practices were different across the communities. In Trackton, for example, reading was done for a purpose, for example, children read manuals to know how to mend their bikes. Heath noted that 'dependence on a strong sense of visual imagery often prevented efficient transfer of skills learned in one context to another'.

If the education system doesn't recognise and take account of the ways in which children have developed their early literacy, then their further development may be impaired.

Activity 65

Read the extract below from Heath's study of some early experiences of literacy in the children of the Trackton community.

1 How is written language meaningful to the children of the community?

2 How do these early experiences of literacy compare with your own memories of experiencing written language?

In the home, on the plaza, in the neighbourhood, children are left to find their own reading and writing tasks: distinguishing one television channel from another, knowing the name brands of cars, motorcycles and bicycles, choosing one or another can of soup or cereal, reading price tags at Mr. Dogan's store to
5   be sure they do not pay more than they would at the supermarket. The receipt of mail in Trackton is a big event, and since several houses are residences for transients the postman does not know, the children sometimes take the mail and give it to the appropriate person. Reading names and addresses and return addresses becomes a game-like challenge among all the children, as the school-
10   age try to show the pre-schoolers how they know 'what dat says.'

Pre-school and school-age children alike frequently ask what something 'says' or how it 'goes' and adults respond to their queries, making their instructions fit the requirements of the tasks. Sometimes they help with especially hard or unexpected items and they always correct errors of fact if they hear them. When
15   Lem, Teegie and other children of Trackton were about 2 years of age, I initiated the game of reading traffic signs when we were out in the car. Lillie May seemed to pay little attention to this game until one of the children made an error. If Lem termed a 'Yield'* sign 'Stop,' she corrected him, saying, 'Dat ain't no stop, dat say yield; you have to give the other fellow the right of way.' Often the
20   children would read names of fast food chains as we drove by. Once, when one had changed name, and Teegie read the old name, Tony corrected him: 'It ain't Chicken Delight no more; it Famous Recipe now.'

*In the USA, traffic signs say 'Yield' where a UK sign would say 'Give Way'.

The role of writing in different contexts: writing for a purpose

Children, like adults, write for a reason. They are aware of the adults around them writing for different purposes.

Activity 66

Compare Sammy's two texts.

a What is the purpose of each text?

b How does the graphology of the text indicate its function?

c In the earlier text (A), how can you tell that Sammy is writing rather than drawing?

Text A: Sammy's shopping list; aged 3 years 5 months, she did this while she was waiting for her mother to get ready to go out and she 'read' the items on the list as she wrote them.

Text B: Sammy's book cover: aged 5 years 4 months, she did this cover for a book of instructions on looking after pets, which she decided to write after she had spent some time playing with her grandmother's cats. She involved her grandmother in the project.

Key: *Pets author Sammy and illustator Granny*

Children understand quite soon that writing is done for a purpose and that different writing had different functions. Before they can understand and interpret the meanings of individual letters and words, they recognise that writing has a distinctive shape and form, and that this shape and form is important to the purpose of the text.

Awareness of connected discourse in written language

Children understand from an early age that whole texts carry meaning.

Activity 67

Read the transcript of Josie reading her book below and discuss the following questions in groups.

1 Is Josie reading the text when she is looking at it on her own? If not, what is she doing?

2 How does Josie's understanding of the text develop when her mother reads it with her?

3 How much knowledge of the text does Josie show when she is reading it on her own?

4 She clearly enjoys the book. Judging from the transcript, which aspects of the text do you think she enjoys most?

> **Josie (3 years 10 months) is looking at the book _We're Going on a Bear Hunt_ by Michael Rosen. She's familiar with the book, which is one of her favourites. She is turning the pages at random. The words she says do not link with the words on the page she has open when she is talking.**
>
> Josie: <singing> Choo, choo choo, choo, we going going going (5) bear hunt bear (3) Oh no! We going going going (6) going (2) uh oh. Wishy wishy wishy (5) Uh oh! <Her mother joins her>
>
> Mother: Have you finished already?
>
> 5   Josie: Mmm
>
> Mother: Shall we read it? Come on. (1) Sit up here. (3) We're going on a bear hunt. We're going to catch ... what?
>
> Josie: A big one.
>
> Mother: A bear?
>
> 10 Josie: A big one!
>
> Mother: Yes. A big one. What a beautiful day. No, not yet. We're ...?
>
> Josie: (shouts) We not scared!
>
> Mother: We're not scared. /Uh oh
>
> Josie: /Uh oh (.) River
>
> 15 Mother: What's that?
>
> Josie: Grass
>
> Mother: Grass. Good girl. Long wavy grass. We can't go (.)
>
> Josie: Under it
>
> Mother: Over it, we can't go (.)
>
> 20 Josie: Under it (.)/Oh no! wishy wishy wishy
>
> Mother: /Oh No! We've got to go through it. Swishy /swashy swishy swashy
>
> Josie: /wishy wishy wishy

Josie is clearly aware of the ways in which written text can form a coherent whole – in this case, in a story she enjoys and in which she can participate.

Independent research

Watch Michael Rosen performing _We're Going on A Bear Hunt_ on his website www.michaelrosen.co.uk/forchildren_videos.html. How does he make use of children's awareness of signs in his reading?

Awareness of the processes involved in interpreting written and spoken language

Children develop understanding within a context, for example, a cereal packet may only convey meaning to a child if the specific cereal (or a similarly packaged one) is part of that child's experience. Parents often report that children will refuse to eat a supermarket 'own brand' because the packaging tells them that this is not their familiar cereal, even though the content might be identical.

Activity 68

Each of the examples of writing below is targeted in some way at young children.

1 Discuss the ways in which a young child may understand the texts and the meaning they might draw from them.

2 Which is likely to communicate meaning earliest and why? What meaning is likely to be communicated?

Text A: from the front of a breakfast cereal packet aimed at children

Text B: from a reading book written for young children

Text C: from a picture book aimed at children under 5

How might a child interpret a text that is about writing, rather than a text that has a clearly identifiable function? The signs on the cereal packet help the child to identify it – they serve a naming function. The story book has a narrative function. The reading book is self-referential. It only exists because reading and writing exist.

Vygotsky's research into children's language identifies the importance of context and meaning. He observed that social interaction is central to language development and thought. A child's early literacy activities are relevant to the child – they have a function – even if the adult is not able to recognise these activities as literacy. As with spoken language, the whole is more important than the part. Evidence suggests that children understand the meaning of a text before they can read or write in the formal sense.

What is a child doing when he/she starts to write?

There comes a point when a child starts to identify letters with meaning and distinguish between their drawing and writing. The basic concepts a child brings to their earliest experiences of literacy are that:

- print carries meaning
- print is different from drawings
- speech can be encoded in print
- print can be read out loud
- print has direction (in English, left to right).

Writing and reading are not translating and deciphering. When children begin to write, they are not simply copying from adult models. It is a process of learning and exploration that can be observed by looking at children's early writing.

Ferreiro and Teberosky carried out some experimental work on the development of literacy. They suggested that progress in literacy 'does not come about by deciphering or copying, but comes about through a long developmental process during pre-school years, from initial conceptions about print to the final sophistications and understandings about function, form and convention.'

It is a recognised phenomenon of spoken language that children will develop forms that are not part of the adult system in the process of language acquisition and will be very resistant to correction. For example, Sammy, aged 3, experimented with a question form 'What because?', which resulted in utterances as her language developed such as 'What can he can't walk because?' She chose eventually to discard this in favour of the standard form, but this was when her own developing system of grammar began to exclude it as a possible option.

In early literacy, a child is also experimenting with signs – in this case, visual symbols that create meaning. This experimentation leads to an understanding of how the system works. Research suggests that children understand about writing, they understand the way it works before they are competent practitioners of the skill.

Phonology and early writing – the development of spelling

When children enter the education system (and frequently before this), they start to learn about the link between sound and symbol, between **phoneme** and **grapheme**, and start to understand that certain symbols represent certain sounds. In a language such as English, where the link between the phonology of the language and the spelling is complex and often counter-intuitive, this is a challenging process. Do you tell a child 'k' is for knee or 'n' is for knee?

Current educational policy focuses on the teaching of **phonics**, using multi-sensory tasks including songs, stories and rhymes. The aim of these programmes is to ensure that children understand the link between grapheme and phoneme in a carefully planned sequence. Written language is seen as a form of code. Children learn how to decode and encode it. They are taught to blend phonemes (merge individual phonemes together into whole words) and to segment words (split whole words into individual phonemes). They are taught that **blending** and **segmenting** are reversible processes: words can be put together and they can be taken apart.

Children are introduced to phonemes and the corresponding grapheme and **digraph** (letter combination) until they are familiar with the 42 main sounds of English and the letters associated with them. The first set of graphemes and digraphs taught is:

The following tables show the correspondence between phoneme and the spelling that children are taught in the early stages of learning to read and write.

s a t p
i n m d
g o c k
ck e u r
h b f ff ll ss

Consonants							
/b/	<u>b</u>at	ʤ	<u>j</u>et	/s/	<u>s</u>un	ʃ	<u>sh</u>op
/k/	<u>c</u>at	/l/	<u>l</u>eg	/t/	<u>t</u>ap	tʃ	<u>ch</u>ip
/d/	<u>d</u>og	/m/	<u>m</u>ap	/v/	<u>v</u>an	θ	<u>th</u>in
/f/	<u>f</u>an	/n/	<u>n</u>et	/w/	<u>w</u>ig	ð	<u>th</u>en
/g/	<u>g</u>o	/p/	<u>p</u>en	/y/	<u>y</u>es	ŋ	ri<u>ng</u>
/h/	<u>h</u>en	/r/	<u>r</u>at	/z/	<u>z</u>ip	ʒ	vi<u>s</u>ion

Vowels							
æ	ant	eɪ	rain	ʊ	look	ɜː	hurt
e	egg	Iː	feet	aʊ	cow	eə	fair
I	in	aɪ	night	ɔɪ	coin	eɪ	dear
ɒ	on	əʊ	boat	ɑː	farm	ʊə	sure
ʌ	up	uː	boot	ɔː	for	ə	corner

Activity 69

Look at the examples below of early spelling by children aged between 4 years and 5 years 6 months. The children are in their first year of formal education and they have been taught to break words down into phonemes in order to spell them.

Try to identify the links they are making between phoneme and grapheme.

a Try to explain how the children have arrived at the spellings. (The chart above might help you.)

b The children are all from Yorkshire. Try to identify any instances where a child's accent might have influenced their spelling.

c 'They've made a lot of mistakes.' Discuss this comment. How useful is it to think of these spellings as 'errors'?

Text A

Key: What shall I see? A cow eeting hai (What shall I see? A cow eating hay.)

Text B

Key: I am goowin on a train ride. Wot shal i see ?? (I am going on a train ride. What shall I see ??)

Text C

Key: Kipper hrd a noys (Kipper heard a noise)

These children are early writers and are applying the knowledge they have to a system that is new to them. They have worked out spellings from what they have been taught. It's unhelpful to think of these spellings as errors, unless they are thought of as the written equivalent of 'virtuous errors' (see page 51). They represent part of the learning process and they show that the children understand the link between sound and letter, and the way the spelling system works.

Writing in imaginative play

Children very quickly transform their world by creating signs out of the items in their environment. A cardboard box can be a car, a boat, a den – whatever the child's imagination can transform it into. As they become more aware of writing, this can become part of the world of their imaginative play.

Activity 70 Read the following account of Bethany, aged 3 years 10 months, playing in her grandmother's office. She has seen people answering the phone and asking for information. She has also seen her grandmother making notes and working at the computer.

What has she understood about the functions of written language?

> **Context: Bethany sits at the desk and picks up a ruler.**
>
> Bethany: This is my tend (pretend) phone.
>
> Grandmother: Who are you going to phone?
>
> Bethany: Shop <*talks on her phone*>. Er Can I have carrots and … carrots and Readybrek. That's Sammy's
>
> 5   Grandmother: OK. Is it Mrs Bethany?
>
> Bethany: It's Bethany! <*She picks up a pencil and starts to 'write' on a piece of paper.*> It's for Daddy.
>
> Later on the same occasion, still playing at 'offices', she uses the keyboard and types letters at random. She finds the letter 'b' and types 'bbbbb'. She says, 'Make it B for Bethany.' She is shown
>
> 10   how to use the shift key and types 'BBBB'. She then asks, 'what does it say?'

Writing in early education

Children aged under five start formal learning of the writing system as soon as they start school. They have to acquire a very complex system, but many children are already aware of a range of systems of signs (logos, pictures, environmental writing) and are able to extract meaning from them.

- They need to know what writing looks like and understand that marks on a page relate to spoken words and carry meaning.
- They need to understand that there are lots of symbols and they can be combined in different ways.
- They need to realise that they can communicate in this way too, but there are conventions that need to be followed in order to make this new code work. These conventions include letter forms, use of capitals and lower case, **directionality** (left to right in English), spacing between words and punctuation.

They need to understand that the variation on letter forms they see in the world around them – B b B B b b b B – can't be extended to the point of inverting them, for example, 'b' and 'd' are different letters.

- They need to understand that the function of the text may influence its form and content, for example, lists run down the page, headings run across and are separate from the main text, crosswords contain one letter in each box.

Writing doesn't only involve understanding. It involves the development of motor skills and the practical tasks of pen control. In the very early stages of writing, children will ignore direction and fit their writing anywhere on the page that suits them. For example, in Activity 64, Bethany has fitted her name across the bottom of her sticker picture, with the letters rising up towards the right-hand side as she runs out of space.

Early writing also shows the beginnings of letter formation. The early texts above both contain letter-like shapes. Sammy's shopping list (text A in Activity 66) shows repetition of patterns, circles with crosses in them and also forms that look like the letter 's', the first letter of her name. Even at this early stage, it is possible to see that the writing goes from left to right. She has also written the items running down the page, showing that she has observed lists being written by an adult and has imitated what she has seen.

Key terms

- directionality

- linearity

Activity 71

Texts A–C below come from a set of drawings representing the writing of a small group of children from the September they first started school in Rising 5s to March the following year. Texts A–C are responses to the topic 'My Holiday News' and were done early in the school year.

Text A: by Josh, who told his teacher 'I played with George', produced in September at the start of the school year

Text B: by Daniel, who told his teacher 'I went on my Dad's surfboard', produced in September at the start of the school year

Text C: by Laura, who told her teacher 'I went to the beach', produced in October

Read the commentary below and discuss the questions in small groups. Do you agree with the commentaries? Do you have any further observations?

1 How are these children understanding the basic concepts of writing (see page 82)?

2 What are they communicating with their writing?

3 Is this writing or drawing?

4 Does it carry meaning for the child?

5 What have the children understood at this stage about the conventions of writing?

Commentary

All three children understand that speech can be written down. They have told their teacher what their images 'say'.

Josh hasn't yet separated writing from drawing, but he has created meaning in his
5   drawing. There is a definite head, face, body and legs.

Daniel understands the purpose of writing. He had drawn an illustration and labelled it. He hasn't understood about linearity, but he does understand writing has direction. He has written his words up the page. Letters from his name can be identified – 'd's, 'i's and 'l's are all there.

10   Laura has a clear concept of what writing is. Hers had directionality and linearity, there are clear letter formations and she has grouped them into 'words'. She is starting to understand about spacing. She is also using upper and lower case letters. She uses her drawing to tell her story as well – there is a child, a flower and a ball.

15   Laura and Daniel have understood that combinations of symbols carry different meanings. They have not yet mastered the system.

Activity 72

The next set of texts from the same group of children as in Activity 71 were produced in January of the following year. They were all written in response to a story about Kipper. The phrase 'Kipper's Toybox' was written across the paper, and therefore modelled for them by the teacher.

Working in groups, answer questions 1–5 as in Activity 71, then explore questions 6 and 7.

1 How are these children understanding the basic concepts of writing?

2 What are they communicating with their writing?

3 Is this writing or drawing?

4 Does it carry meaning for the child?

5 What have the children understood at this stage about the conventions of writing?

6 What developments can you identify in the children's writing?

7 All these children live in a small, largely working-class town and are local to the school they attend. They have been taught by the same teacher. Decide whether their development of writing skills are at the same level. Suggest reasons why/why not.

Text A: *sfsc*

Text B: *Kipper throod awt his toys and cawt his toys Kipper hrd a noys*

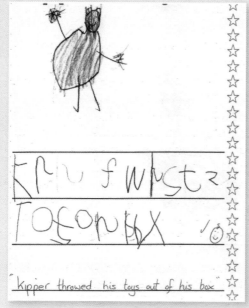

Text C: *kpr fw hz tz to fo his bx*

Activity 73

The final set of texts by the same group of children are taken from the end of the first school year. **Text A** from Activity 69 is part of this set and you can include it in your discussion if you wish.

How are the children handling the conventions of written English now?

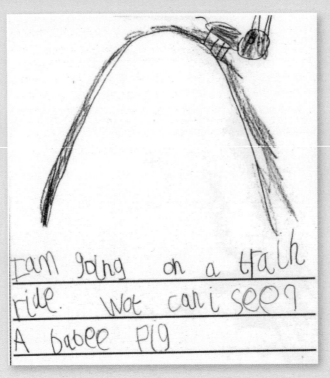

Text G: *Iam going on a train ride. Wot can i see? A babee pig*

Text H: *I am going on a train ride. Wot can I see? Sum ginee pig*

The next stages

Once children have begun to develop the skills of writing, they apply them in a range of ways. They will continue, in a school context, to 'write for the sake of writing' – an activity which may well have little real meaning for a child who is used to their activities having a context and a function. They will also use written language for a range of purposes: to write letters and notes, to write cards, to write notices, to produce lists, to express themselves.

At very early stages, as you have seen above (see page 76), children understand that they can do things in writing that they cannot do with speech, for example, send messages over a distance in time and space (letters, notices), name and label things, record and report. Some of their writing reflects the way they use spoken language – it tends to be personal, colloquial and context-bound, with a high use of 'and' as a coordinator (a common feature of spontaneous spoken language).

However, even these very early examples of writing have differences from what you might expect to find in children's spoken language.

Independent research

You might like to refer to the speech-writing continuum you studied for Unit 1 (AS Student Book, pages 13–21). To what extent do children distinguish between written, spoken and multi-modal forms of language?

Activity 74

Read the texts below, written outside of the classroom context. Working in groups:

1 Identify features that you think are unlikely to occur in the children's spoken language. Remember that because spontaneous spoken language takes place in real time, it tends to use a series of clauses that are more commonly linked by coordinating conjunctions (and, but) or simple subordinating conjunctions (so, cos), and context-bound forms such as **deictic words and phrases**.

2 How are these texts different from texts that were produced in a classroom context? (See the texts in Activities 71–75 and 77.)

Key term

• deictic words and phrases

Text A: story by S., aged 5

This is a wich woo has caught a clown and she has stuk a nife into the clown. Why she mixis the majic powrs to kill the funny clown. She is killing him just becuse he
5 is funny. But there was a resun why she is going to kill the funny clown becuse she dusunt like funny things and all clowns are funny and speshaliy that one. Evry onn liked him but that wich. Evun the other
10 wichs loved him delly. They all thut he was gret exept for thet one woo was the only wich in the wuld woo didunt like funny things. She relly did hate funny things. But evry body loved them. and that is the end of
15 the story about the wich and the clown.

Text B: story by P., aged 6 (spelling has been corrected)

Long ago, before motor cars were invented there was this little boy and his name was John and this boy named John liked to go in the forest to see his grandparents and on this particular day he was walking through the forest when, just
5 when he walked through a clearing of four trees, a giant net sprang on to him. The next thing he knew was that he was flying to a nearby cave by the claws of a bat. When he got to the cave he told them everything to let him go. He told them of his father's psychology work. He told them that his father
10 could make laser beams. So they let him go and the king of the animals, who was, of course, the Lion roared 'Show this great laser beam of yours to me!' and the boy said 'I will' and went off home. He told his father about what the Lion had said. After the talk the father did let him have the laser beam.
15 When the boy was in the Lion's cave he threw the laser beam to all the animals and what a fright the animals got when it blew up and the boy and his father lived very happily ever after. The end

The differences between children's written and spoken language becomes more marked as their skills in writing develop and they begin to make linguistic choices that differentiate between spoken and written forms.

Activity 75

Compare transcript A, of a child's spoken language, with text B, an example of a child's early writing. What differences can you observe between Marcus's written and spoken language?

Transcript A: Marcus (6 years 3 months) is telling his class about a trip to the seaside he made with his family in the holidays.

Teacher: What did you do next, Marcus?

Marcus: An (.) an we went to (.) we went (.) the sea and we played wiv (.) wiv the ball an we (.) had a picnic then we (.) Dad said it's time to go and we (.) we got in the car and we drove home.

Text B: Marcus's account of his day at the sea

Key: *Look there is the sea. Shall we play with the ball? Let's eat our food. Everybody put your seatbelt on. Let's go. We will stop to go to the toilet. Come back in <??>*

Activity 76

Read text A below, written by 7-year-old Maya. This is an account of an earthquake that hit her home city of Sheffield.

1 Is Maya's account more or less context bound than Marcus's in Activity 76?

2 What devices is she using that are available to a writer, but not to a speaker?

Text A

Key: *The … earthquake! In the night!*

In speech bubbles:

Frame 1: *Whoooo!*;

Frame 2:
a) *Mummy mummy the house is moving*;
b) *No it is not go back to sleep*;

Frame 3:
a) *I think you were right on the news it said there was an earthquake*;
b) *Told you!*

A pore mans chimney fell down; My mum did not bleeth [believe] me.

Activity 77

Read Texts A and B below, which are two stories written by Sammy at home, ten months apart, without any prompting to carry out a written task. On both occasions, she decided she would write a novel (her grandmother is a novelist).

Note: Text A shows the first two pages of Sammy's first story; the remainder of the text has been represented in type.

1 How does Sammy structure narrative?

2 How are they different from the way she might tell these stories if she was speaking?

3 Is she using any devices to create atmosphere, describe scenes, develop characters?

4 What genres have influenced Sammy's writing style, in your opinion? What features of her text suggests these to you?

5 How is she handling the conventions of written English?

6 Can you identify changes in her writing between the two texts?

Text A The thing made out of blood, by Sammy (7 years 3 months)

Key: ***The thing made out of blood Chapter one: The family***

Violet had two sisters and a brother. Her two sisters were called Sharlotte and milley. Her Brother was called Adam. Violet was an <??> Like her two sisters and brothers.

Violet was good. In fact her brother and sisters were good. One sunny day there was as Violet
5 *expected 20 pressent's. They were for Her. It was her Birthday. She was 10. She had got a camera, telly and lots of other stuff. 'Wooh.' She said. It was the best birthday she had ever had.*

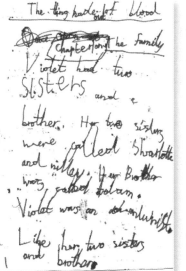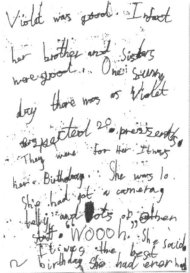

The text continues (spelling, punctuation and capitalisation are presented as they were written, but other aspects of the text are not reproduced here):

Chapter two: The red drip

Violet was walking to school. She suddenly Remembered that she had forgotten something. She plodded back to the house. There to her Right she saw a red drip, She ran inside and told her mum. 'Mummy Mummy I saw a red drip!' said violet 'Oh did you Violet!' said Violets Mum. 'Yes I did!' Shouted Violet. 'For that shouting I wil not bother with it. Said Violets Mum. Violet didn't bother arguing. She Just picked up her school books and off she went.

Chapter 3: The thing made out of blood

After school Violet went home. She was going to play tig with Marcus. He was a friend of Violets. They played tig till Marcus had to go She went to bed She saw a thing made out of blood …

Text B: The Bloodriper (Blood ripper), by Sammy (8 years 1 month)

Key: *The Bloodriper*

'There is a bloodriper in town! Esta said to Sharn? 'How did it get in town'? Asked Sharn. 'I don't know'. Said Esta. 'Lets find out' Sharn, 'Yes.' Lets find out. So the two girls went and started there quest. (Note the page number 1 at the bottom left of the page.)

They serched the town. Moving quietly encase the bloodriper came out.

* * *

There was a sudden movement in the bushes. Esta froze sharn fainted. 'Are you allright Sharn.' 'Yes.' 'Look over there Esta'. (Note the page numbers 2 and 3.)

Popular culture, new media and digital literacy

In the 21st century, children live in a world of multimedia texts. They experience film, television, print, computer games, video and console games, mobile phones and the Internet. They are aware of and participate in electronic forms of communication like emails, texting and SMS messaging. They also play games, using platforms such as Playstation, Nintendo and XBox. Language is changing and developing in response to a rapidly changing and developing world, and our concepts of literacy, and the ways in which we try to develop these skills in children, needs to change and develop as well.

Kate Pahl has carried out research into the ways in which console games allow children to explore a range of textual practices in relation to the contexts provided by the games. Console games provide a form of narrative structure, but unlike the narrative provided by a book they present the child with a series of challenges – puzzles they must solve, skills they must master, tasks they must perform – before they can move on to the next stage of the narrative. As the child plays the game, they also project themselves into the game, becoming an 'I' who is participating in the action.

Games frequently move between the world of the game console, the world of the television and film (e.g. the Beijing Olympics were covered by a console game that some children played during the same time period the games were being televised; many games are spin-offs from popular TV series or films) and the world of children's play. It is reasonable to expect that these worlds also appear in the narratives that children tell and write.

3 Tackling Section B of the exam

There are two questions in section B of the exam. The texts will be drawn from the language of children of a various ages and stages in the acquisition process. The data may represent the child at a certain age or may represent the child's language over time. The texts could be drawn from spoken language, written language, or both.

Question 2 (a)

This requires a relatively short response to a specific piece or pieces of short data. The text could illustrate written or spoken language. The question will ask you to focus on a specific aspect of the data relating to children's language features you have studied and you will have to identify, describe and comment on the selected feature. You will need to use linguistic terminology to describe the characteristic key features of the aspect of the text you have been asked to analyse, relate it to context and make reference to relevant theories to support your exploration.

Question 2 (b)

This requires a longer essay-style response and will be based on additional, longer pieces of data. Again, the data could be spoken or written language. The examiner is looking for evidence that you can make links between the textual features found in the material, their context and how they relate to the theories you have studied.

> ### Writing in the exam
>
> Having studied the theories, in the exam you need the ability to select relevant features, concepts and theories. You will never be asked to write about theories and research, but to apply those that are appropriate. You should always aim to 'attach' your explanation of theories to specific examples in the text.

Assessment objectives

Question 2 (a) is worth 10 marks. They are split between:

AO2 Demonstrate critical understanding of a range of concepts and issues related to the construction and analysis of meanings in spoken and written language, using knowledge of linguistic approaches **(4 marks)**, and

AO3 Analyse and evaluate the influence of contextual factors on the production and reception of spoken and written language, showing knowledge of the key constituents of language **(6 marks)**.

Question 2 (b) is worth 40 marks. These are divided as follows:

AO1 Select and apply a range of linguistic methods to communicate relevant knowledge using appropriate terminology and coherent, accurate written expression **(10 marks)**

AO2 (15 marks), and

AO3 (15 marks)

Activity 78

1 Read the sample Section B 2 (a) question.

2 Study the guidance in pairs, and identify how the sample response meets the criteria for AO2 and AO3.

3 Identify other aspects of Louise's written language in texts A and B that you could identify and analyse to meet the criteria for AO1 and AO2.

SECTION B: CHILDREN'S LANGUAGE DEVELOPMENT

Read texts 1 and 2 and answer the following questions.

Both written texts were written at home. Louise (age 5 years, 2 months) chose to write them as part of her play.

2. (a) Identify and analyse **two** ways in which Louise is making the link between phoneme (sound) and grapheme and/or digraph (letters).

1. ....

....

....

2. ....

....

....

TEXT 1

a handwritten Christmas message written 2 weeks after text 2 without help from an adult

Key: *To Gramor I hop you hav a nighs Krismis (To Grandma I hope you have nice Christmas)*

TEXT 2

This text was written 2 weeks before text 1. It was written on a computer while Louise was talking to her grandmother. Louise inserted the image herself.

> **louise's chryismis pich owvumth**
>
> **this is a very very prity presit.**

Key: *Louise's Christmas picture album. This is a very, very pretty present.*

Suggested approach to question B 2 (a)

- Find two different examples of the way in which Louise makes a link between sounds and letters. You won't be credited if you repeat the same point twice. Louise has obviously already made clear links between sound and letter, and will have started learning about this at school.

- There are a lot of examples you could choose, but it's important that you identify more than the fact the Louise had spelled a word correctly or incorrectly. Examples might include: Krismis/Chryismis, pich, nighs, hop, hav, owvumth, prity.

- When you have identified the examples, you must explain and analyse them. For example, you could discuss the different ways certain sounds are represented in spelling and the way in which Louise had identified these. You could also identify the way certain sounds in non-phonetic alphabets are represented by more than one grapheme, for example, her spelling of 'nice' as 'nighs'.

Sample response for question B 2 (a)

Children are introduced to phonemes and corresponding graphemes in the early stages of learning to read and write. Louise will have been taught that the phoneme /I/ is represented by the grapheme 'i', in words such as 'hit', 'list', etc. She has made the reasonable assumption that this is how the /I/ sound of 'pretty' is written. This is not the conventional spelling of the word, but it shows that Louise has understood how phonemes and graphemes are connected, and she has made best use of the knowledge she has.

Louise knows that some sounds are represented by letter combinations, digraphs. She has used the digraph 'ch' to create the sound /ʧ/ and uses it in 'picture'. This probably represents Louise's pronunciation of the word as /pi, ʧ/. She omits the spelling of the final schwa /ə/. In the early stages of writing, children often represent the consonant sounds and omit the phonemes.

Suggested approach to question B 2 (b)

Look at all three texts and analyse them to identify as many different aspects of the development of Louise's written language as you can. You will need to explain why such features are present and relate them to the context. You will also need to identify relevant theory and discuss it in relation to the data. One of the texts is constructed in the process of discussing it with an adult. You will need to look at the ways in which the spoken language helps or hinders the construction of the text, and the ways in which the adult uses language to guide the child through the process.

You need to cover a range of points in order to achieve highly when answering this question, including:

- the function of the writing, and the indications in theories that children write for a purpose

- the differences between the piece Louise produced on her own and the piece she wrote with her grandmother's help: this would be a good place to look at Vygotsky's theories of the zone of proximal development

- the way in which Louise is using the conventions of written English, including spelling (you can expand on points you made in question 2 (a)), linearity and directionality, letter formation, spelling, punctuation, the form of the text and its relation to its function

- the differences between her electronic text produced on the computer and her handwritten text

- the role of her grandmother in helping her to write

- her grandmother's use of child-directed speech

- Louise's intentions in the text and her grandmother's perceptions of Louise's intention.

Activity 79

Read the sample Section B 2 (b) question below.

1 In pairs, use the guidance to write an essay plan, with detailed notes.

2 On your own, write an answer to the exam question, in essay form.

SECTION B: CHILDREN'S LANGUAGE DEVELOPMENT

2. (b) Using texts 1 and 2 (from question 2 (a) on page 94) and text 3 below, discuss the ways in which Louise's written language is currently developing and the influences on it. What role does the spoken language have in the construction of text 2?

TEXT 3:

Louise (L), aged 5 years 4 months, talking with her grandmother (T-Nanny) as she wrote text 2 on the computer

Key: text between / / indicates the use of a phonemic symbol < and > represent overlapping speech

T-Nanny: What have you put?

Louise: Louise

T-Nanny: Ok

5 Louise: mm

T-Nanny: Well can you write something about the photo what's the photo of?

Louise: Um lemme just do this

T-Nanny: Let me just put it (.) the thing after Louise <*sound of typing*> so do you remember what the photo was of?

10 Louise: Well (3), this is about Louises is /uː/w/ɪː/s /ɪ/z /ɪː/z/

T-Nanny: <mmhmm

Louise: ok, well I have to go ba ba back <*typing*>>

T-Nanny: oh Louise's yeah, so you want that apostrophe, that little comma thing, and then an 'S' after it.

Louise: /sə/

15 T-Nanny: /sə/

T-Nanny: Right Louise's

Louise: It sounds like a /ɪ/

T-Nanny: yeah (1) Louise's what?

Louise: K /kɜː/ Where's K /kɜː/? Is it a curly /kə/ or a kicking /kə/

20 T-Nanny: for what (1)

Louise: I'm writing Christmas

T-Nanny: Christmas is a curly /kə/

Louise: /kə/

T-Nanny: And then there's actually an 'H' after it//

25 Louise: /kr/>

T-Nanny: <a bit like ch /tʃ/. It's a silent 'H' (2) and then an>

Louise: </kr/

T-Nanny: /r rə/

Louise:		</kr/
30	T-Nanny:	/r rə/
	Louise:	/krɜː/
	T-Nanny:	/kr ə/
	Louise:	/ɪ/
	T-Nanny:	mhmm, /s/
35	Louise:	/mə/
	T-Nanny:	mhmm
	Louise:	/ɪ/
	T-Nanny:	mhmm
	Louise:	/sə/
40	T-Nanny:	mhmm (1) Louise's Christmas (1) and who is with you in the picture, or what was your present?
	Louise:	I mean, I want to write this
	T-Nanny:	mhmm
	Louise:	Louise's Christmas /pəː/ (2) /pəːɪ ch ʧ/ picture
45	T-Nanny:	mhmm
	Louise:	picture
	T-Nanny:	yeah
	Louise:	Al
	T-Nanny:	put another space (2)Louise's Christmas Picture
50	Louise:	/aʊ/ A /aʊ/ sound is /ɑː/ and a /wə/
	T-Nanny:	Very good
	Louise:	/ɑː/ /wə wə/ <??>
	T-Nanny:	/wə/ at the top
	Louise:	/aʊ/ /vɜː/ (1) /vɜː/ where is /vɜː/?
55	T-Nanny:	</fə/?
	Louise:	/və/
	T-Nanny:	/bə/?
	Louise:	no /vɜː/
	T-Nanny:	/vɜː/ is at the bottom
60	Louise:	/aʊ/ /və/ /aʊ/ /və/ /ɪn/ /aʊvəm/ /ʌ/ /aʊlvʌm/
	T-Nanny:	Alvum
	Louise:	Alvum
	T-Nanny:	so /ʌ/
	Louise:	/ʌ/ /mə/
65	T-Nanny:	mhmm. Louise's Christmas Picture Album /aʊvʌm/ <laughs>

Unit 4: English language investigation and presentation

For Unit 4, you will complete two tasks. The first task is an article, a talk or a presentation introducing your investigation topic; the second task is an investigation into an aspect of English language that you have chosen to study. The two tasks are linked. Task 1, the article, talk or presentation, will form part of your preparation for Task 2, the English language research investigation.

What you will do in the course

To carry out Task 1, you will:

- identify an audience you want to address
- choose which format you want to use
- read widely around your topic area
- produce a written text appropriate for your chosen audience and format.

Using the information you have gathered from the first task, you will then carry out an independent research investigation into the topic you have chosen, adapting it in the light of any feedback you received from Task 1.

In order to carry out your investigation (Task 2), you will:

- plan your programme of study
- select a topic area
- decide on a research question
- devise a methodology for researching your topic
- collect appropriate data
- apply your knowledge of the **key constituents** of language to your data
- analyse it using suitable tools
- apply and test appropriate theory
- make appropriate critical judgements about your area of study, supported by your research findings.

How you will be assessed

There is a maximum of 80 marks for this unit, 24 marks for Task 1 and 56 marks for Task 2. Task 1 is assessed through AO1 (6 marks) and AO4 (18 marks). The most important aspect of this task is your ability to write in a way that is suitable for your audience and your chosen format. Task 2 is assessed through AO1 (10 marks), AO2 (16 marks), AO3 (16 marks) and AO4 (14 marks). All assessment objectives are important for this task.

Writing your coursework

In your coursework folder, you will have:
- One piece of writing for Task 1, 600–750 words (24 marks)
- One piece of writing for Task 2, a report, 2000–2250 words (56 marks)
- References and bibliography for Task 2
- Appendix containing all your raw data for Task 2.

	Assessment objective	What this means in practice
AO1	Select and apply a range of linguistic methods to communicate relevant knowledge using appropriate terminology and coherent, accurate written expression	You should: • Identify a suitable method for researching your chosen topic. • Apply it effectively and accurately. • Use the appropriate terminology accurately. • Present your final investigation in a report that is coherently structured and easy for the reader to follow. • Write clearly and accurately.

Assessment objective		What this means in practice
AO2	Demonstrate critical understanding of a range of concepts and issues relating to the construction and analysis of meanings in spoken and written language, using knowledge of linguistic approaches	You should: • Identify language concepts and issues (e.g. gender, power, social and cultural variation, change over time) that are important to your topic area and your research question. • Apply appropriate linguistic approaches. These could include **sociolinguistic theories**, **psycholinguistic theories**, **pragmatics**, **semantics**, among others. The key is to use these in a way that will help you answer your research question. • Show that you understand the significance of your research results.
AO3	Analyse and evaluate the influence of contextual factors on the production and reception of spoken and written language, showing knowledge of the key constituents of language	You should: • Show that you understand the context of the language you are investigating. • Apply the relevant key constituents in a way that is appropriate for your research question.
AO4	Demonstrate expertise and creativity in the use of English in a range of different contexts, informed by linguistic study	You should: • Demonstrate your ability to apply linguistic theory in an independent piece of research. • Show you have a clear understanding of your chosen topic. • Communicate this information clearly in a way that is appropriate to an informed reader in a report format.

How to succeed in Unit 4

• Be open-minded about language – don't embark on your research with pre-conceived notions.
• Spend time on the preliminaries: topic choice, deciding on a research question and devising a methodology.
• Use Task 1 to help you with the preliminary stages.
• Ask the people around you for support: ask your teacher for expert advice and discuss your investigation with other students.
• Stick to your timetable.
• Be painstaking – take enough time with each stage of the work you do.
• Present your final work according to the guidelines.

Key terms

• **sociolinguistic theory**
• **psycholinguistic theory**
• **pragmatics**
• **semantics**
• **key constituent**

How to use this book

Unit 4 of this book can either be read from start to finish and used as a guide to help you with your research investigation, or it can be dipped into so that you identify and use the sections that are most relevant to your own specific investigation.

Section A: Approaching your coursework is relevant to all coursework investigations and will help you to choose a topic area that suits your interests and expertise. It also gives you advice on managing your time and setting a realistic schedule for your work.

Section B: Task 1 takes you through the process of completing Task 1, and using this task to help you to refine and focus the topic you have chosen to research.

Section C: Task 2 explores different ways research topics can be approached, the types of research you can carry out, methods of collecting different types of data including collecting spoken and written language, designing and using questionnaires. It also gives advice about ways in which data can be analysed. This section is one you should use selectively. It will give you advice on a wide range of collection and analysis methods, but not all of these will be relevant to all investigations.

Section A: Approaching your coursework

In this section gives you guidance and advice on how to start your research investigation. This means learning how to ask suitable questions about language, and how to decide on a topic that will interest you and lead to a successful piece of research.

1 What is research?

Research is a way of finding out answers to questions. It is organised, systematic and involves the collection and analysis of data. In order to carry out a research investigation into an aspect of the English language, you will need to identify a topic you wish to research and a question you want to answer. You will collect and analyse data in a way that will give you an answer to the question. This section will take you through the first stages of this process.

During the time you have been studying it, you will have observed aspects of language closely, analysed them, studied theories about language that other researchers have developed and formed your own ideas and opinions. There will be areas that you have found more interesting than others. There may be areas the course has only looked at briefly that you would like to explore further or there may be areas you have studied more closely that have left you with questions that you want to answer. Your own observations of the language you hear around you will have led you to develop ideas of your own about the way language works. The best investigations often arise from these observations of language behaviour.

Research questions

Research begins with a question. The research question is one of the most important aspects of an investigation because it will become the driving force behind your research. It will dictate what data you collect and what methods you use to analyse it. The conclusions of your investigation will form an answer to this question. Whatever topic you decide to research (see Choosing your topic below, page 106), you will need to identify a research question relating to it.

This section looks at ways in which research questions can be identified and formulated. A good research question needs to satisfy certain criteria:

- It must not be too broad or general.
- It should not have already been answered by previous research (although it is perfectly acceptable to expand or test existing research).
- It ought to provide a useful answer.
- It must be 'do-able', that is, it must be a question that can be answered through means that are available to you.

Some research questions are so big that they could (and do) occupy the time and attention of well-resourced research centres for decades. Others may have been comprehensively answered already, so that there is no original research to be carried out. Some are simply not useful (a question to ask yourself is: Who wants to know this, and why?) and some would be almost impossible to explore using experimental means.

Across AS and A2

You have already had experience of working with language data and analysing it in Unit 1. You explored the key constituents of language and learned how to identify the ones that are significant for specific aspects of a text (**field**, **function**, **tenor** and **mode**). You also carried out some independent research for Unit 2: collecting **oral narrative**, interviewing, and collecting information for a presentation.

Key terms

- field
- function
- tenor
- mode
- oral narrative

Activity 1

Here is a list of research questions that were used for A-level English language investigations. Each investigation achieved very poor marks because the corresponding question has a problem that led to serious difficulties later in the research process. Can you identify the problem in each case and suggest a solution?

1 How do children acquire language?

2 What are the origins of the place names in my area?

3 What is the difference between the language of gardening magazines and the language of fashion magazines?

4 How can you tell when people are lying and when they are telling the truth?

5 Are there identifiable differences in the language used by writers of literary novels and the writers of popular fiction?

'What are the origins of the place names in my area?'

'How do children acquire language?'

Exploring a research question

Thinking about research in the abstract can be confusing. The following activities will allow you carry out a brief language investigation and look at ways in which research questions can be focused and explored.

A word that has recently appeared in the English language is 'nahmean', a shortened form of 'Do you know what I mean?'. Before a new word can be included in the *Oxford English Dictionary*, certain things need to be established about it: how long has the word been in use, what it means, where it comes from, what class of word it is, the forms it takes. All of these can be considered as research questions.

Activity 2

1 Find examples of 'nahmean' in text or in spoken language. Look in music magazines and rap lyrics, listen to casual conversations and interviews, particularly with bands, and explore the internet. Remember that the spelling may vary. How many different spellings can you find? Make a list of the kinds of texts (spoken, written, electronic) where the word was used. Who uses this word, in what context and why?

2 Look in the *Oxford English Dictionary*. Is the word 'nahmean' (or any of the spelling variations you have found) included? If not, is it included in any other dictionaries, for example the online Urban Dictionary (www.urbandictionary.com)? If a word is not in the dictionary, how can you identify the meaning?

3 Using your own examples, and texts A–C, try to answer the following questions about this word. Which ones can you answer by studying the data and which ones need further research?

   a What are the origins of the word 'nahmean'? Where was it first used?

   b Can you identify any other words in the English language that have been formed in a similar way? Are these recent or have they been in the language for a long time? (Try looking up the etymology of blackbird and daisy in the *Oxford English Dictionary* or refer to Section A: Language diversity, page 8 in Unit 3.)

   c What word class is it?

   d How long has it been in the English language? Is it likely to become a permanent addition?

   e How many alternative spellings have you identified?

   f In which social contexts does this word appear? Who uses it?

Text A: The Boondocks

THE BOONDOCKS © 2000 Aaron McGruder. Dist. By UNIVERSAL PRESS SYNDICATE. Reprinted with permission. All rights reserved.

Text B: Interview with Part 2, New Flesh for Old

Extract from a 2000 interview with the white hiphop artist, Part 2. The interview was published on the internet and is transcribed directly from the tape but some features of spontaneous spoken language may have been omitted for clarity. (Big Dada is the name of a recording company, New Flesh for Old is the name of the crew, Part 2 is the name of the artist.)

So lets set the scene … errrm well actually theres nothing to set. I'm sitting on the settee in my house trying to sellotape up a mashed dictaphone – getting not very far n' showing the sort of skills which made me realise Blue Peter weren't really gonna be knocking down my yard to drag me off for fame and charlie snorting fortune. So bring on the New Flesh For Old. First up the brains behind the beats within the organisation – the founding geezer of NF4O from back in '92 … Mr Part 2

You've been around putting out vinyl since around '94 yeah?... I was wondering why it took so long from '97 when you released the Electronic Bombardment 12″ and like it took two years later since 'Eye of the Hurricane' came out?

It costs a lot of money nahmean n' the first 12″s we done ourselves – and after we signed to Big Dada (in 1996) at that time they weren't really doing albums n' that cos they had just set up the label n' were only doing 12″s to build up the label. […] And I'm also talking about doing a New NF4O album as well – which is going to be a New Flesh International LP … so it's going to be a lot broader and is going to break away from the UK … the UK rap labelling-type of thing cos it's universal music nahmean n' I'm gonna be pushing it a bit more widespread. But anyways Big Dada are definitely doing albums now that they got it properly off the ground.

Nice – were you happy with the way 'Equilibrium' sold?

Aye – yeah it's not bad. It's an improvement cos when we first started out in the UK scene people were just pressing up 500s.

Speaking about walking – how did the recent UK tour go … how was you received out there?

It was received really well … but some of the media people were taking the piss nahmean.

Text C: Blog advertisement

http://www.philtown.com

October 14, 2005

THE BIG FIVE, NAHMEAN

There are five numbers that we have to look at to determine whether a business has a Moat. Moat, of course, is some sort of protection by which a business automatically wards off competitors.

5 Protection comes in a lot of flavors. Some bad boys protect their urban businesses with tech nines, nahmean. But we don' be investin' dere, bro, nahmean? We gonna move up to a better class of management that does their fighting with their brains, not their bullets. It's a lot safer and has a much more consistent success rate.

10 So we want some sort of **Brand** (when you want a Coke, a Pepsi just won't do), **Secret** (patents and trade secrets), **Switching Cost** (too much hassle & expense to switch from Windows to a Macintosh), **Toll Bridge** (can't advertise to all of Washington, D.C. without buying ad space in the Post), or **Low Price Moat** (Walmart).

15 Any of these offer protection without a lot of fighting. No tech nines. Just an occasional lawyer. **The Big Five numbers are a clue that there is a big Moat in place.** And if the Big Five are bad, ain't no moat, bro. You want to defend that castle you better count your ammo, nahmean?

20 The Big Five are just:

1 Return on Invested Capital (ROIC); and the growth rates for

2 Equity

3 EPS

4 Sales

25 5 Free cash

We want to see all of these at 10% or better and not dropping.

www.philtown.com/phil_towns_blog/2005/10/the_big_five_na.html

Your data and the data provided give a lot of information about 'nahmean'. The word itself and its use, its meaning and its word class, and in this case, the etymology can be worked out quite simply. The spelling has clearly not been standardised yet. There are two alternative spellings in the data provided and the data you have collected may offer other examples. The data also gives some information about the contexts in which the word is likely to be used.

You would need to carry out further research using dictionaries and texts from the last 10–20 years to find out how long the word has been in use in the English language. You would also need to do further research to support your original theories about the contexts in which the word is used before you could draw valid conclusions about this.

The actual origins of the word 'nahmean', in the sense of where it first appeared and who first used it, are probably not recorded and therefore not possible to identify.

By answering the first two questions in Activity 2, you have just carried out a short research investigation into a word that is a recent addition to the English language. The answers to the questions came from an analysis of the data and some basic research into secondary sources (dictionaries, online dictionaries, texts containing the word).

You have also explored several related questions (in question 3) to see which ones could be answered by further research. Some could be answered relatively easily, for example, the class and structure of the word. Other questions required further detailed research: the word's sources, its current status and the social contexts in which it is used.

The activity also identified questions about the data that it is not possible to answer without the resources of a big research institution and questions that it is not possible to answer by observing or experimenting (also called empirical research).

When you identify a topic you think would be suitable for your investigation, a preliminary exploration of the area will help you to formulate and refine your research question.

'Nahmean' investigation: topic area, language change/diversity ➜ word stock ➜ individual word ➜ 'nahmean' ➜ questions (origin, meaning, spread, context, etc.)

2 Choosing your topic

What is your investigation going to be about? What language topic would you like to research? One of the most important things about topic choice is to select something that you find interesting so you can maintain motivation through a process that will occupy you for several weeks.

You have probably found some areas of language study more interesting than others and may already have decided that you want to carry out your investigation into one of these areas. A useful starting point is to organise your thoughts using a personal questionnaire to identify your interests and your other areas of study. English language investigations often link in with other subjects (after all, you use the medium of the English language to study them) and work done for them can be used to enhance your understanding. The following questionnaires were completed by students who were planning their A-level English language investigations.

Personal questionnaire

Student A

Personal interests:
sport (football), computer games, journalism

Other subjects:
psychology, media studies, sports studies

Language issues arising from these:
sports commentaries, motivational language, media language, newspaper language

Areas covered by the course that interest me:
electronic texts, language

Student B

Personal interests:
music, creative writing, folklore

Other subjects:
French, sociology

Language issues arising from these:
translation, stylistic analysis of literary text, the language of cultural traditions

Areas covered by the course that interest me:
children's writing, narrative writing, the way people tell stories (oral narrative)

Activity 3

Below is a list of possible investigation topics drawn from Student A and Student B's interests. The topics have been written in the form of initial research questions.

Student A	Student B
Psychology, media studies and sports studies	**Children's writing and creative writing**
The language of sports trainers: How does a trainer use language to motivate trainees during a coaching session?	**Children's narrative writing:** What narrative techniques do children use when they start writing stories? (1)
Political uses of sports language: How is sporting achievement used by politicians for political gain?	**Children's writing and sociology**
Sports studies and language change	**Children's writing and social group:** Is there a link between social group and the development of writing skills? (2)
Sports commentary over time: How has the language of sports commentary changed over time? (1)	**Narrative writing and folklore**
Attitudes to women in sports language: How are changing attitudes to women shown in the language of sport? (2)	**Oral narrative:** Are there identifiable patterns in the structure of oral narratives? (3)
Media studies, journalism and language change	
The language of newspapers over time: How has the language of newspapers changed over the past 50 years? (3)	

Do the numbered research questions fulfil the criteria for a good research question as discussed on page 100? Evaluate them using the table below.

Criteria	Student A questions			Student B questions		
	1	2	3	1	2	3
It must be focused and precise.						
It should allow for original research, that is, it is a question that has not already been answered or fully explored.						
It ought to provide a useful answer.						
It must be 'do-able', that is, a question that can be answered through empirical means.						

You will probably have found that each of the research questions needs further refining before it can be used for an investigation of the kind required by this course. This is not a problem. Almost all research questions need refining as an investigation progresses. If you can see ways in which this can be done at this early stage, then the investigation is moving along the right lines.

Certain questions, however, need treating with caution: for example, questions that can't easily be refined, that already seem to be answered, that don't seem to be leading in a useful direction, or that seem at this initial stage to be very hard to investigate.

Activity 4

1 What narrative techniques do children use when they start writing stories? This research question covers a very large area. It can be broken down into smaller, more focused questions:

- How does one child's narrative writing develop over a 6-month period?
- What is the range of narrative skills among a group of 6-year-old children in the same class at school?
- What narrative devices can be found in the stories written by a group of children of the same age?

2 Choose another of the research questions from Activity 3 and break it down into a series of more focused questions. Which one do you think would make the best language investigation?

Activity 5

1 Working in pairs, discuss your personal interests, the other subjects you are studying and aspects of English language study that arise from these. Fill in a questionnaire like the one below. (Don't worry if you haven't covered the aspects of English language study that particularly interest you in your course yet. You can study them at the same time as you carry out an investigation.)

Personal interests:

Other subjects being studied:

Language issues arising from these:

Area(s) covered by the course that interest me:

2 Compare your questionnaires. See if you can identify any links between your areas of interest, your personal interests and/or the other subjects you are studying. These interests open up a range of topic areas from which a final investigation topic can be drawn.

3 Make a list of topics that interest you. Write them in the form of questions. You now have a list of topics from which you can choose to identify one that you will follow to carry out your investigation.

4 Test your topics against the criteria for good research questions.

- Check with your teacher that the topics seem feasible for an investigation. (See Activity 3)
- Talk about the topics with other students.
- Check that you will be able to collect data for each possible investigation.

The process in Activity 5 will allow you to eliminate any topics that may not be appropriate or that may present difficulties later on. You will be left with a short list of topics that are suitable for research investigations. Choose the one you want to pursue.

You are now in a position to begin your investigation.

3 Managing your time

Good time management can make coursework enjoyable and allow you to achieve to the best of your ability. A bit of planning will take a lot of the stress out of the process.

When you begin a research investigation, you will have a deadline for completing the task – a deadline when your Unit 4 folder must be handed in. You should set yourself a deadline for completing a first draft that will give you time to edit and rewrite where necessary.

The length of time between the start of the investigation and the deadline for your final submission will be set by your school or college. The important thing for you is to find out when your deadline is and how many weeks you have been given so that you know how long you have to write your investigation.

If you manage your time properly, you can create a schedule that will make the whole process less stressful and give you a clear idea, early on in the process, whether you are keeping up to date, are ahead of where you need to be, or are falling behind. If you identify that you are falling behind as soon as it happens, it's easy to catch up. If you are seriously behind and don't realise it, then you will have to rush your work. One of the major reasons for an investigation not achieving as highly as it should is because the writer didn't give him/herself enough time to carry it out.

Your deadline date is your target. You need to identify important milestones on the way. In a research investigation the milestones are:

- identifying a topic and a research question
- completing Task 1 (including a literature review, focusing the research question and exploring research methods)
- choosing a research method
- collecting data
- preparing and analysing the data
- drawing conclusions from the analysis
- writing up your results.

Aim to complete a first draft of your investigation two weeks before your deadline to allow you to make any last minute changes and put a final polish on your work.

Drawing up a realistic schedule

The following section is based on a centre that gives its students fourteen weeks to produce the first draft of an investigation and a further two weeks to produce the final draft. If you have a schedule like that, you may feel that you can relax a bit. Sixteen weeks may seem like a long time to write a 2000–2250-word research investigation. Planning your timetable may give you a different picture.

> **Key term**
> - Sample

Activity 6

1 Read the milestones identified by Student B, who carried out a research investigation into the structures of oral narratives collected in a South Yorkshire mining village.

1 Identify a **sample** of 30 informants.

2 Collect and record one narrative from each informant.

3 Write the first draft of methodology.

4 Transcribe narratives.

5 Analyse data.

6 Write up the first draft of findings.

7 Write the introduction and conclusion.

8 Produce the first draft of the investigation.

9 Read it. Edit and rewrite any unsatisfactory sections.

10 Submit the investigation.

2 Now identify the milestones for your own investigation.

Activity 7

Using your own deadline, plan your timetable and see exactly how much time you have. Use a diary and calculate the number of weeks you have been given. *Your* first milestone is identifying a topic and a research question. You need to put your milestones into your diary at regular intervals between now and your submission date.

Making adjustments

Each investigation will require different lengths of time for each milestone.

Activity 8

1 In small groups, discuss the requirements of each investigation:

- Is your data collection going to be time-consuming or simple?
- Are you going to need a lot of time to familiarise yourself with your data?
- Will you need to collect your data in two or more stages? (see Student D's investigation pages 131–132)

2 Make adjustments to your milestones, within the fixed points of your start and end dates, to reflect the investigation you are carrying out.

Sticking to your timetable

Below is one week in the diary of a student doing three A-levels. Each subject has six hours of class time each week, spread across two classes. One class session in each subject will be used for coursework for one term. The student also works and has football practice. There is also a week's holiday within the timescale that will give a period clear of classes. Saturday afternoons and Sundays have been left clear of allocated time, but are available for catching up if the schedule starts to slip. This means the diary is sufficiently flexible to allow for unexpected events along the way.

	Monday	Tuesday	Wednesday	Thursday	Friday	Saturday
Morning	English class	English investigation	Psychology class	Sociology class	Psychology class	Work
Afternoon	English class	Coursework period for catching up with deadlines	Sociology coursework	Sociology class	Psychology coursework	
Evening	Football	Work	Homework	Homework	Free time	Free time

Activity 9

1 Using your diary, write in all your commitments, including classes, work and fixed engagements between now and your final deadline.

2 Decide which times you intend using to work on your investigation. Remember, you may have other coursework to fit into this schedule. The times that you have allocated for your investigation should be treated like class time or work time – not available for other things.

Setting a schedule like this should ensure that you know exactly what is happening to your time when you are working on your investigation. If you have any unavoidable engagements in that time, you will be aware of them and be able to adapt your timetable accordingly. Make sure you have enough flexibility so that if you do start falling behind, you have time available to catch up.

Good planning can make the difference between an A or a C grade, or a C grade and a fail.

Having decided on your topic area, you should begin Task 1, which will help you to refine and focus your research question.

Coursework milestone

At this stage you should:

- know what your topic area is
- have an initial research question
- have your diary completed with milestones and deadlines clearly indicated.

Discuss this with your teacher to make sure you are on target.

Section B: Task 1

In this section you will learn how to write on an academic topic for a selected audience. You will learn how to write articles, posters, talks and presentations, and show that you can explain aspects of your topic area to people who are knowledgeable about language but not about the topic you have chosen to investigate. You will also develop your understanding of your topic area and refine your research question.

Task 1 gives you the opportunity to explore your topic area in detail and prepare for your English language investigation. You will write a short article, talk or presentation of between 600–750 words about the area of study you have chosen for your research. You will write this for an 'informed but non-expert' audience. You will need to demonstrate that you can write in a way that is appropriate for the format you have chosen, and that you can explain your chosen topic area and research question to a group of people who are well informed about language but may not be familiar with your topic area.

This task will form part of the preparation for your language investigation, as well as being a separate piece for assessment in its own right. For Task 1, you will:

- select an appropriate audience
- explain your topic area
- explain your research question
- explain the reason you have chosen it.

Assessment objectives

Task 1 is assessed through AO1 (6 marks) and AO4 (18 marks). AO1 marks are awarded for your skill in selecting material that is appropriate for your subject, chosen format and audience; presenting a final text that is accurately written, coherently structured and easy for the reader to follow.

AO4 marks are awarded for showing you have a clear understanding of your chosen topic area, communicating this information clearly in a way that is appropriate for an informed but non-expert reader and for the format you have chosen.

1 Linking the task to your investigation

In order for a language investigation to be successful – to carry out meaningful research and achieve a good grade – the preparatory stages of the investigation must have as much focus as the later stages. If the topic choice and research question are flawed, the whole investigation will be flawed. A very common mistake is to rush these early stages because you are aware of tight deadlines and want to make quick progress towards the final piece. The early stages include:

- topic choice
- identifying a research question
- refining the research question
- reading widely around the topic.

Task 1 is designed to help you with the important early stages of a research investigation. One of the best ways to develop an understanding of something is to explain it to someone else.

Before you begin Task 1, you should have identified your topic and have some ideas about your research question. You now need to expand your knowledge of this area by:

- carrying out a literature search
- carrying out some preliminary fieldwork
- discussing your plans and ideas with your teacher.

Carrying out a literature search

Research is a bit like building a wall. Each row of bricks is supported by the rows below, and the structure of the new row will be dependent on the previous structures. When you carry out research, you are dependent on the people who have researched your area before you. You need to see what other people did, what they found out and what they learned in relation to your research question. Read as widely as you can around your topic and your research question. This will help you to narrow your focus and also to decide on the research method that is suitable for your topic.

Use the best library you can access – your school or college library, your city library, the library of your local university – and read the relevant sections of the most up-to-date books you can find. The most recent research will be published in journals. Try to identify the ones that are most relevant to your topic – your teacher and your librarian will be able to advise you. Use the internet. This is a valuable resource, but remember that information on it is not reviewed and not all information on websites is accurate.

Preliminary fieldwork

You are researching an English language topic. For many topics, the raw material for your investigation is all around you. What you observe – the language behaviour – is as valid as the observations the theorists make. Preliminary observations with your research question in mind will help to familiarise you with your topic area and help you decide on ways to collect the data you plan to use for research purposes.

Activity 10

Linguist Robin Lakoff claimed that women's language has the following characteristics, among others:

> **Women …**
>
> * use super-polite forms (would you mind, I'd appreciate it if … etc.)
> * use 'empty' adjectives (divine, lovely, etc.)
> * avoid coarse language or expletives
> * use hyper-correct grammar and pronunciation (prestige forms).

Observe the casual language of your peers and spontaneous spoken language on TV (e.g. in a reality show like *Big Brother*).

* Do your observations support Lakoff's claims?
* Which ones do they support? Some? All? None?

If your preliminary fieldwork shows that the language you are observing doesn't behave in the way that theorists have led you to expect, don't dismiss this. Incorporate it into your investigation preparation and use it in your findings if your data supports your initial observations.

2 Selecting an audience

What is an 'informed but non-specialist' audience? You are looking for an audience that has a good understanding about language issues, but may not be experts in the topic area you are investigating. This means that you don't need to explain general language issues (such as the definitions of key constituents, key concepts or the speech/writing continuum), but you may need to explain issues that are specific to your topic area or your research question. You could write for:

- English language and humanities students
- teachers
- readers of English language journals targeted at school teachers or A-level students
- an adult audience who have an informed interest in language issues.

The audience you choose will often depend on the topic you have chosen.

3 Choosing a format

You have a choice of three formats: a talk, a presentation or an article.

- A talk is a spoken presentation given directly to an audience. It may be supported by handouts or other visual aids.
- A presentation is a multi-media format that can use spoken and written language and also graphic devices. It can be delivered via the spoken voice using slides in a format such as PowerPoint (in which case it is very similar to a talk) or it can be a poster presentation, delivered as a written and visual display with the writer present to discuss and answer questions.
- An article is a written piece delivered to an audience that is not present.

Your choice of audience and format will affect your choice of style and **register**. Presentations and posters on academic subjects are usually formal, although any spoken format will need to indicate an awareness of the audience's presence. Articles may be less formal, depending on the kind of publication you plan to write for.

Key term

- register

Across AS and A2

Presentations and articles were options for your AS coursework. These were written for a different purpose and targeted at different audiences, but you will use and adapt the skills you developed for your Task 1 piece.

Activity 11

Working in groups, discuss the topic areas each of you plans to investigate, including the advantages and disadvantages of each format for each topic area.

- What are the advantages of having your audience present?
- Is a spoken delivery better than a written one?
- What about a 'crossover' format such as a poster? It must stand alone (i.e. be as informative as it needs to be without any additional material), but it is useful to consider what questions people reading your poster might ask you.

Talks

The talk requires you to show that you have an understanding of a specific topic area and can explain this to an audience who have a general understanding of the issues around English language study, but who may not be familiar with your topic area or the specific aspect of your topic area identified by your research question.

The talk needs to be very clearly structured. As you deliver your talk, your audience will need clear guidelines to make sure they know what it is to be about, what the main topic of each section is, how it links to the main topic, how it links to what has already been said, and where it is moving to next. Remember that the audience for a talk can't stop and go back to review something. They depend on you as the speaker to give a very clear delivery and explain each unfamiliar concept (or indicate clearly that this will be explained at a later point).

Planning your talk

To start planning your talk, write down a list of the important points you want to make – the message you want your audience to take away with them. This list will be quite short, no more than four or five points.

Once you have your list, your talk should focus on these points. The outline for your talk should look something like this:

- Introduction
- Point 1
- Point 2
- Point 3
- Point 4
- Conclusion.

The introduction should establish the overall topic in its wider context and give a brief outline of the rest of the talk so that the audience know what is coming, including important background material they will need to understand the talk. It will introduce the main points in the order in which they will occur in the talk. Each point should follow on logically from the previous one. You can also offer your audience 'tasters' to let them know what is going to come later on, which will help to maintain their interest.

Activity 12

1 Read the notes student B wrote as part of planning a spoken presentation.

Topic area: Children's early writing

Research question: How does a 4-year-old's awareness of writing develop over a six-month period?

Audience: a group of A-level English Language students

Introduction: What is writing and how do children experience it?

Point 1: Emergent writing – what it is and how a child uses it

Point 2: The way a child's awareness of the environment helps to develop reading and writing

Point 3: Writing for a purpose – why children write

Point 4: The things that influence a child's developing writing

Conclusion

2 Now read the introduction to the talk below.

> Today I want to talk to you about children's writing. I want to study the way one child's writing develops over a six-month period. Most people think that writing is something children learn at school. From reading about the subject I have found out that most children are
> 5 producing a form of writing – often called emergent writing – long before this. I've brought some examples to show you, but before I say any more about it, I'd like to explain to you about signs and how they work. Signs are systems of meaning and everyone uses them, including small children, from quite an early age. They will very quickly
> 10 become familiar with logos and things like that before they understand about writing. It's important to understand that children are producing a kind of writing before they actually produce real writing.

3 Can you link the introduction with the notes? A good introduction will explain:

- what the talk will be about
- the main points that the speaker plans to talk about
- signpost clearly when the speaker is moving from one topic to another.

4 Using the tips above, rewrite the introduction to improve it.

Once you have produced a plan, you should follow it. An introduction can move ahead and give 'tasters', but it's very important that this doesn't lead to a confusing structure where the audience don't really know where the speaker is going.

The main body

Talk about each of your points in turn, in the order you have already introduced them. Keep it clear and at a level that is suitable for the expertise of your audience. Use slides or other visual aids to clarify a point or to demonstrate what you are talking about.

Activity 13

Read the following section from student C's talk on the development of pragmatic skills in children's language. The talk is aimed at a group of parents who have been attending a family learning course that demonstrates ways in which they can help their children develop language. They therefore know a lot about the way small children use language, but they aren't aware of much of the theory underlying the area. This section is the student's introduction, leading into the main topic.

- How does this speaker let her audience know she is moving on to a new topic?
- How does she link her new topic to a previous one?
- How does she engage with her audience?

> I'm going to talk to you about the ways in which children develop the skills of conversation. Any parent of a three-year-old will know that children love to talk, but where does their language come from? When a child is born, it has little or no knowledge of language.
> 5 It lives in a world of sound, vision and touch, and it has to make sense of this in the best way it can. Some linguists believe that a child is born with an innate capacity for language development,

10 while others believe that language is acquired through imitation and reinforcement. Both groups agree that in order for a child's language to develop successfully, a language environment is essential so that the child is exposed to the sounds, vocabulary and grammatical structures of their language. When you consider that a child has no conception of these, it seems amazing that by the time they reach school age, they are competent communicators.

15 But as well as the meanings and structures of language, a child must learn to use language appropriately in different social settings and also develop the skills of conversation. These skills are complex and advanced. Think about what you do when you hold a conversation. You have to introduce a topic, obtain the listener's attention,

20 understand about **turn taking**, respond to what other people say, use the right address forms and politeness markers, make indirect requests, recognise potential breakdown of conversation and make repairs or request clarification, use persuasive tactics and manipulative devices, as I'm sure you have noticed.

25 One aspect of children's conversation is that they use a lot of questions.

Conclusion

It is useful at this stage to recap your main points to summarise your presentation. It can be useful to have your main points on a slide at this point, just to make sure that your audience has got the message.

Key term

• turn taking

Activity 14

Read the conclusion to student C's talk below. Is it effective? How does she:

- sum up what she has said?
- link her conclusion to the main body of her talk?
- recognise the presence and the expertise of her audience?

So as I have tried to explain, I think that children use questions in conversations in a different way from adults. I think that by studying these, it will be possible to learn a lot more about the ways in which children acquire – or fail to acquire – those very important social skills

5 of language. I think anyone who has had experience of young children will know – if there's one thing they are good at, it's asking questions. Thank you for listening. I'll be happy to answer any questions.

Presentations

Presentations can either be spoken or poster presentations. A spoken presentation will always have a visual element: PowerPoint slides, sound or video files, or overhead transparencies. The script that goes with these will have the same qualities as a talk and requires the same skills to write. It is important that in a spoken presentation, you refer to the audio or visual material you are presenting as well.

WHAT IS EMERGING FROM THIS TEXT PRODUCED BY A CHILD AGED 5?

Children:
- use images combined with letters to represent meaning
- show understanding of the relationship between sounds and symbols, even in 'mistakes'
- display their familect – influence from the language around them
- use writing for various purposes: to be loving, humorous, idiosyncratic.

Poster presentations

Poster presentations are often given at conferences or events when there isn't time for every presenter to give a talk. A poster is a static, visual means of communication that gets your points across to a group of people as quickly as possible. Posters also allow you, as the presenter, to engage your audience in discussion and answer questions.

Posters use images and short blocks of text, but they need a carefully planned overall structure if you are going to communicate your message to your audience.

To start planning a poster, you should write down a list of the important points you want to make, in the same way as for a talk (see page 115). These points represent the message you want your audience to take from your poster. Each point should be expanded into a block of text with graphics that will support it if necessary. Your introduction should summarise the whole of the poster – this is what the poster is about.

Remember – posters use visual grammar. A poster displays the essential content – the messages – in the title, main headings and images. It indicates the relative importance of elements graphically: each main point is stated in headings, using a large type size; details are subordinated visually, using smaller type. The structure of a poster is:

- Title – the main, overall point
- Introduction – an overview of the topic, including a concise account of your research question, the aspect of the topic area you plan to investigate
- Main points – one section each and visually equal, using the same type size, approximate length and font
- Conclusion – suggestions for way forward and questions that arise from the issue you have raised. (There isn't any need to summarise a poster. It's there for your audience to read.) This section will be useful to you for any further refining of your research question.

A good poster will:

- use headings to summarise the main points
- organise the material so that the reader is led through the text
- give clear visual signs about the level of importance of each point.

Articles

Articles, like talks, presentations and posters, need careful preparation and clear structuring. A good starting point, if you are planning to write an article, is to look at the work of professional writers who are writing for the kind of audience you are targeting.

The opening of your article is very important. It needs to engage the reader's interest from the opening line. A reader needs to know what the article will be about and that it is appropriate for them, and the topic needs to be presented in a way that will engage their interest.

Independent research

Look at instructions for writing academic posters on the internet at www2.napier.ac.uk/getready/writing_presenting/academic_posters.html#structure or look at some examples at www.ncsu.edu/project/posters/NewSite/ExamplePosters.html. Remember that most academic posters show research results. In contrast, you are producing a poster to show your initial ideas, rationale and planning.

Activity 15

1 Read the following openings for articles that appeared in *emagazine*, a magazine that is produced for teachers and students of English language. Note how each writer takes a very different approach, even though the audience is the same.

2 How does each writer:

  a draw the reader into the article?

  b tell them what it will be about?

3 How does each article address its audience? Can you identify:

a the level of **formality**?

b the ways in which the writer engages the readers' attention?

c the ways in which the overall topic of the article is introduced?

4 Which article did you want to read further? Why?

Key term

• formality

Text A: Buffy: a pragmatic slayer

Q: How do you address a thousand-year-old vengeance demon?

A: Very, very politely.

Talking to a vengeance demon isn't an everyday conversational situation for most people, unless they happen to be characters in the hit TV drama series *Buffy the Vampire Slayer*. The writers of this programme have set themselves a range of challenges that the writers of a soap, for example, don't have. Not only does this series have to represent realistically the rhythms and style of American teen-speak, they have to handle conversational contexts that are, to say the least, unusual.

Danuta Reah

Text B: Language at full stretch

For many centuries dictionaries and grammars of the English language have taken the written language as a benchmark for what is proper and standard in the language, incorporating written and, often, *literary* examples to illustrate the best usage. Accordingly, the spoken language has been downgraded and has come to be regarded as relatively inferior. What is written and what is literate is accorded high cultural status. Even dramatic performances are often valued and studied primarily as *written* text. When spoken language has been preserved, it is in the form of transcribed 'text' which, as we can see on page 21, is often laid out in such a way as to highlight and discredit its 'formless' character.

Ron Carter

Text C: Shakespeare's false friends 4 – being rude

If someone says to you, 'Don't be rude,' you've done one of two things. Either you've been daringly impolite – like putting your tongue out at someone. Or you've been rather indecent, having just said a naughty word or told a dirty joke.

Rude is quite a common word in Shakespeare. It turns up over 70 times in the plays and poems. What you have to remember is that it is *never* used in the modern sexual usage, and hardly ever in the impolite sense either.

David Crystal

Activity 16

1 Read the two versions of the article overleaf. They represent the first and final drafts (not necessarily in that order) of a short article written by student B who carried out an investigation into the structures of oral narrative.

2 How is the audience addressed in each version?

3 How is their 'informed' awareness of language made use of?

4 How is the topic introduced and explained?

5 Which do you think is the final version and why?

Independent research

Read the complete articles in *emagazine*, December 2003. Identify the ways the articles are structured and the different ways they address an 'informed but non-specialist' audience.

Version A

We all tell stories. Every culture and every society has its collections of folk narratives and traditional stories, but we also tell each other stories in everyday situations. We talk about what we have been doing, we talk about things that have happened to us and we tell jokes.

These stories, oral narratives, are part of our everyday life. They aren't the carefully thought-out stories found in fiction, but stories told spontaneously as part of our day-to-day interaction.

The content of oral narrative will vary from group to group, but is there an underlying structure, a 'grammar' of narrative that is universal to all or most oral narratives? Several theorists working in the field of narrative claim that such patterns exist. The Russian Formalist Vladimir Propp identified an underlying grammar in a set of fairy tales, William Labov claimed to have found evidence of such a structure in the narrative patterns of New York City street gang members, Roland Barthes claimed that all narratives shared a limited number of structural features and the folklorist Axel Olrik identified a law governing folk narrative that can often be found in more elaborate oral narrative.

Do these patterns exist in the stories we tell today? In order to find out, a small collection of oral narratives could be made and analysed as a starting point, and the different patterns the theorists claim to have found would have to be applied to these. If the patterns appeared, then this would be evidence that these patterns still exist. The potential for future research would be enormous.

Version B

'The weirdest thing happened to me the other day...' 'My mate told me that his friend's brother...' 'There was this man, you see...'

Do you recognise these? Has anyone ever said anything like that to you? Can you guess what comes next? You may not be able to say exactly, but most people realise when someone starts talking like this that they are going to hear a story.

We all tell stories. Story-telling in something that people do. Along with language, story-telling seems to distinguish us from other animals. Before human societies developed writing, they used stories to keep their cultures and beliefs alive. A lot of these stories have been written down and come to us in collections of folk tales and fairy stories. Most people believe that we don't have folk stories of our own, that our culture has grown beyond this. But is this true? Maybe the stories we still tell each other – 'You'll never guess what happened to me last week!' – are more like folk stories than we realise.

If this is true, then some of the content and some of the structures that have been identified in folk narrative may be found in modern oral narratives. How do the narratives open and how do they close? Who takes part in them? What points do they make, if any? When are they told? What are they about? These are all valid questions for a researcher to ask, and the only way to find the answers is to observe oral narrative in action.

Version A is more academic and moves straight into theories and the focus of the investigation, the idea that there may be identifiable structural patterns. Version B places the academic background in a more familiar context, which may be helpful for the reader to understand the point of the research.

Coursework milestone

Check your diary. Are you on target with your current milestone? At this stage you should have:

- carried out a literature search
- carried out preliminary fieldwork
- identified the format you plan to use for Task 1 and the audience you wish to address
- started writing your Task 1 text.

Section C: Task 2

This section gives advice and guidance on how to:

- carry out independent research,

- decide on a research process,

- collect and analyse data,

- draw relevant conclusions from what you find, and

- structure and write a report.

Task 2 is a research investigation. You will carry out an independent piece of research into an English language topic of your own choice and write it up in a report format of 2000–2250 words.

At this stage you will have identified your research topic and used your work on Task 1 to identify problems with the initial stages. You should now know that your topic is 'do-able', you should have carried out some preliminary reading and observation and you should have some ideas about how your research question needs to be focused and refined

Assessment objectives

Task 2 is assessed for all four Assessment objectives:
AO1 (10 marks), AO2 (16 marks), AO3 (16 marks) and AO4 (14 marks).

AO1 marks are awarded for your skill in identifying a suitable research method for your chosen topic and applying it effectively and accurately, using the appropriate terminology accurately, presenting your final investigation in a report that is accurately written, coherently structured and easy for the reader to follow.

AO2 marks are awarded for your ability to identify language concepts and issues (e.g. gender, power, social and cultural variation, change over time) that are important to your topic area and your research question, and to apply appropriate linguistic approaches. These could include sociolinguistic theories, psycholinguistic theories, pragmatics and semantics, among others. The key is to use these in a way that helps you answer your research question. You also need to show that you understand the significance of your research results.

AO3 marks are awarded for showing that you understand the context of the language you are investigating and that you can apply the relevant key constituents in a way that is appropriate for your research question.

AO4 marks are awarded for showing that you have a clear understanding of your chosen topic area, communicating this information clearly, in a way that is appropriate for an informed reader in a report format, and demonstrating your ability to apply linguistic theory in an independent piece of research. (Theory, in this case, means the concepts and ideas developed by other researchers in the field that you have studied during the course or read about in your preparation, or theories you have developed yourself in the course of your study of language.)

1 Focusing your research question

A frequent problem when starting the research for an investigation is that the topic chosen turns out to be too big to be researched within a relatively short time and written up in a relatively limited word count.

Activity 17

Look at the following research questions suggested by students before they carried out their work on Task 1. They realised the topics were far too big and needed to be cut down. The first topic has been done. Try to focus the second and third questions in a similar way.

1 How do children develop conversation skills?

2 What are the differences between literary and popular fiction?

3 How has the regional dialect of my area changed over the past 50 years?

> How do children develop conversation skills?
>
> Child language → children's spoken language → children's conversation skills
>
> **Research question 1: At what age are gender differences apparent in children's conversation?**
> Child language → children's spoken language → children's conversation skills → sociolinguistics → gender → gender in chidren's conversation → emergence of gender differences
>
> **Research question 2: What are the functions of questions in children's conversation?**
> Child language → children's spoken language → children's conversation skills → pragmatic devices → use of questions

If your work for Task 1 shows you that your research question is too large, don't panic. A good research question can usefully be narrowed to focus on a smaller aspect of the topic than you originally planned. A well-focused research question will lead to a better investigation.

Coursework milestone

Check your diary. Are you on target with your current milestone? At this stage you should have:

- identified your topic
- identified your research question
- focused your research question.

2   Choosing a research method

In his book *The Stuff of Thought*, Steven Pinker says that true research does not come from 'Eureka!' (I found it) moments, but at moments when a researcher observes a phenomenon and thinks 'That's funny…' You may be asking your research question because you have seen something about an aspect of language that doesn't fit in with the theory you have been taught (that's funny…). Other research questions may arise because you want to know more about a specific area of language or find out why language behaves in a particular way in a particular context.

These kinds of issues will affect the way you carry out your research: the kind of data you collect, the way you collect it, the way you analyse it and the kinds of conclusions you draw.

Language is a very broad topic. In order to plan your research, you need to make some decisions about the kind of approach you plan to take.

- What is your general approach?
- What is the aim of your research?
- How much control do you plan to have over the **research context**?

General approach

Some research questions are asked because the researcher has noticed an interesting phenomenon in some aspect of language and wants to find out more. The researcher has no theory. The aim is to find an answer to the question. This approach is sometimes called 'question based'. The researcher has observed something interesting about language, but hasn't any theories about what is happening. The aim of the research is to find out more. Question-based research tends to explore issues such as:

- why people use language the way they do
- how attitudes towards language develop
- how situation and context can affect the way people use language
- the language differences between social groups.

Student C's investigation into the functions of children's questions (page 116) and student A's investigation into language change in newspapers (p 107) are both examples of question-based research. The outcome of this kind of research, interestingly, is often a **hypothesis**, which further research at another time can test.

Some research questions are asked because the researcher has a tentative theory – an idea drawn from observation of language or from reading the theories other researchers have developed – that they want to test. This kind of research is hypothesis-based, that is, it tries to analyse the data to test a hypothesis. It is often (but not always) concerned with numbers and measurement in the collection and analysis of data.

A third kind of research is descriptive research, which analyses a variety of language that has not been fully described before or that has undergone some fundamental changes since it was last described and identifies its main characteristic features.

Descriptive research is probably the least commonly found, as it is hard to find varieties of language that have not already been exhaustively described. Examples that have lead to successful investigations include a study of the graffiti produced within a particular cultural group and a study of the messages of congratulations and condolence sent to one woman over a 30-year period on her wedding, the births of her children and the death of her husband.

Another example of descriptive research is a dialect study carried out between 1950 and 1961, *Survey of English Dialects*. This focused on specific dialect words and collected them from carefully selected informants. It produced dialect descriptions from looking at specific key constituents, and some of its findings are still used in language study today.

Key term

- research context
- hypothesis

Independent research

Obtain a copy of the introduction to *Survey of English Dialect*. Read the first two chapters and look at the questionnaire. How useful would this survey be to record current English usage? You can hear some of the recordings from the survey on the British Library Collect Britain website www.collectbritain.co.uk/collections/dialects/

Other dialect studies have collected examples of regional speech in a range of contexts and used them to draw up descriptions of the dialect in question.

Activity 18

1 Working in groups, look at the following research questions. How would a researcher go about finding answers to these questions?

- What are the functions of questions in children's conversations?
- Are swear words relating to religion (blasphemy) still seen as offensive and if so, by whom?

2 Discuss the individual topics the group members are planning to investigate. Which kind of approach would be best for each research question?

Forming a hypothesis

A hypothesis is a tentative statement that proposes a possible explanation for some phenomenon or event. A useful hypothesis is a *testable* statement, which may include a prediction.

A good hypothesis can be very helpful when you are planning your investigation, as it will direct you to the kind of data you need and the best ways of collecting it. In the examples given below, two students have put forward tentative theories about a topic area in language that they want to explore.

- I think British newspapers may be biased against Muslims.
- I think that oral narratives told by different people will show similar patterns in structure and in syntax.

Can these be turned into useful hypotheses? First they could be turned into research questions.

- Are British newspapers biased against Muslims?
- Do oral narratives have identifiable patterns of structure and syntax?

If you have formed your own theory about your research question or if you are aware of theories about language that suggest a possible answer (your literature review will help you here), then in order to research it, you should form a hypothesis. This needs to be more than a statement. A testable hypothesis should be written using the words 'if' and 'then'.

- If British newspapers are biased against Muslims, then an analysis of a range of articles focusing on Muslims should show a negative bias.
- If oral narratives follow a pattern, then this pattern will be identifiable in a range of oral narratives told by speakers in a South Yorkshire pit village.

Activity 19

1 Working in groups, look at your own research questions and decide whether your research is **deductive** (research that will test a hypothesis) or **heuristic** (research that will explore a phenomenon you have observed).

2 If you asked your research question because you have a theory about language, try forming a hypothesis by turning it into an 'if … then' statement.

Key terms

- deductive research
- heuristic research
- circular research

Avoiding common pitfalls

'Circular' hypotheses

Some hypotheses have the potential to form **circular research**. In some cases, the wording of the hypothesis will influence the outcome of the research or the hypothesis is simply stating the obvious.

Activity 20

The following hypotheses, which have not yet been put into 'if … then' format, all have problems.

1 Try to put each one into 'if … then' format. Can you do it? Does this help you to identify the problem?

2 Identify the problem in each case by linking it with one or more of the expert's comments.

Hypotheses

- Right-wing newspapers are biased against illegal immigrants.
- The language of unscripted commentary is different from the language of written sports reports.
- Children brought up exposed to writing will acquire written language in the same way as they acquire spoken language, without any teaching.
- Obscene language is still offensive, even though it's used more often these days.

Expert's comments

- A hypothesis shouldn't contain leading or biased concepts or words.
- This hypothesis contains a subjective judgement. Can you define your data sources more clearly?
- This is a reasonable hypothesis, but it's impossible to research in the time and raises serious ethical issues.
- Isn't this a bit circular? Wouldn't everyone be against something defined this way?
- If the two things are different, you don't need a hypothesis to investigate this. The matter is already decided. You wouldn't try to make a hypothesis from the idea that chalk and cheese are not the same thing.

Independent research

You can get information on the very interesting work done by Susan Savage Rumbaugh on culture and language in Bonobo chimps on www.ted.com/index.php/talks/susan_savage_rumbaugh_on_apes_that_write.html. This has implications for human acquisition of language (see Unit 3).

Forced hypotheses

A hypothesis isn't necessary to all research. Only certain types of research need one. If you have no predicted outcome for your research, then you don't need a hypothesis. For example, student C's comments about children's use of questions in Activity 17 suggests that she does not have a tentative theory about this. She has simply observed that children use alot of questions. To try and force a hypothesis would push the investigation on to a track that may not be useful. Similarly, the investigation into different narrative techniques in prose and graphic novels on page 126 doesn't put forward any theories, it simply demonstrates an interest that student C wants to follow up.

'Off the wall' hypotheses

'Off the wall' hypotheses have no support in the real world of language. Examples from investigations that students have tried to carry out include:

- My dog has language and can speak.
- If you play a recording of someone's spoken language backwards, you will hear what they are really thinking.

Issues around animal language are very interesting and there is a lot of research being carried out into the potential primates have for language. Dogs can clearly communicate with each other and can understand signs and instructions from humans. There is no evidence, however, that the sounds they make are in any way a language.

Reverse speech is a phenomenon identified by a small group of people who believe that when we speak, we subconsciously choose words that, if played backwards, will say what we really mean.

Does it matter if a hypothesis is wrong? Is it a problem if, after carrying out detailed research over several weeks, you find that you have disproved or thrown serious doubt on your hypothesis? No. Research is carried out to test a hypothesis. Proving a hypothesis wrong or doubtful is as useful as proving it probable or right.

Independent research

If the concept of reverse speech interests you, you can read about it and listen to some examples on skeptoid.com/episodes/4105. This will also demonstrate to you why some people may be led to believe in this phenomenon, and why they are wrong.

Key term

- Forced hypotheses
- 'Off the wall' hypothesis
- Reverse speech

Control of the research context

The research context is the environment in which you observe the language you are investigating. For some kinds of research, you will want to observe language as it occurs naturally. For example, if you wanted to investigate the development of children's conversation skills, you would want to record the child or children you were observing in a range of contexts: playing together, talking to adults, and so on, but you would want these conversations to occur naturally.

For other investigations, you may want to manipulate the context to find out how this affects the language you are studying. For example, if you wanted to look at dominance issues in language, you might want to set up a context in which dominance would emerge, such as a problem-solving task that had to be carried out by a group. You may want to vary the situation to see how dominance changes with a different task or with some new participants.

It's useful to remember that question-based research often needs less control over the research environment than hypothesis-based or descriptive research.

Activity 21

Below are some comments students made about the reasons why they chose the research topics they did, followed by the research question they decided on. (There is data available for some examples, see pages 131 and 136.) Work on the questions below in groups.

Topic	Ideas/reasons for research topic	Research questions
1	I'm interested in gender differences in spoken language. I want to see if these can be identified in young children.	Are boys more dominant than girls in group activities at the age of 8?
2	I want to look at the way the language of newspapers has changed over time.	Does the language of newspapers reflect/manipulate the social values of the different periods in history? (see Activity 39)
3	I'm interested in the narrative techniques that writers use to tell stories if they've only got dialogue to work with, for example, in comics and graphic novels.	What are the different functions of dialogue in comics and graphic novels?
4	I've noticed that when young children have conversations they use a lot of questions and I'd like to study this further to see why they do it.	What are the functions of questions in children's language?
5	I don't recognise the gender differences in language that some theorists identify when I listen to my friends talking.	Can gender differences be identified in a group of 17-year-old speakers who know each other well?

1 What is the aim of each research topic? Is it question-based, hypothesis-based or descriptive?

2 Form a hypothesis from each research question.

3 How much control should the investigator have over the research context in each case? Should it be manipulated or should the language be collected in a naturalistic way?

4 Do the students need to refine or narrow any of the research questions further at this stage?

There isn't always one correct answer to questions like the ones in Activity 21. Sometimes the answer depends on the approach you want to take as you carry out your investigation and on the way you like to work. Some topics, however, are better suited to one form than another.

3 Collecting your data

In order to carry out your research investigation, you need data to analyse. Data collection should be carefully planned. You need data that will help you to answer your research question or support (or otherwise) your hypothesis. A useful rule to remember when collecting data for research purposes is:

GIGO: garbage in, garbage out

A research investigation is only as good as its data.

Research subjects

At this stage, you need to decide on your **research subjects** – the actual sources of your data. If you are looking at spoken language, they will be people; if you are looking at written language, they will be texts.

Your subjects will be drawn from a **population**. In research, 'population' refers to the group from which your subjects are drawn, so it is also the group that your subjects represent. Your findings will only be relevant to the specific population you have selected, so you need to be clear about its characteristics. 'Population' can also refer to written texts. For example, in student B's investigation into oral narrative, her population is the inhabitants of the village where she carries out her research. Her sample is the 100 people from whom she collected stories. In student A's investigation into language change in newspapers, his population is all regional and national English newspapers. His sample is the newspapers/articles he selected.

Variables

You also need to be aware of the **variables** that may affect your data. A variable is any measurable characteristic of your data that can take on different values. There are two kinds of variable, **dependent** and **independent variables**.

An independent variable is a variable that stands alone and isn't changed by the other variables you are trying to measure. An independent variable might be age. For example, if you were investigating the language of 4 year-old children, there is likely to be a big difference between a child of 4.1 (4 years 1 month) and a child of 4.11 (4 years and 11 months) and you would need to take account of this. A similar age gap in a group of adults is unlikely to affect the data; you would need a much wider age gap for this to be a variable. Social and cultural group can be another independent variable than can have a significant influence on language.

Dependent variables are ones that change depending on different factors. For example, age (independent variable) will affect the way a child uses language (dependent variable). Social or cultural group (independent variable) may affect the way a person responds to a text (dependent variable). Usually, in a research investigation, you are looking at the ways in which dependent variables change under the influence of independent variables.

Key terms

- research subjects

- population

- variables

- dependent variables

- independent variables

Key term

- Validity

Validity

How are you going to collect your data? The way you do this will affect the **validity** of your investigation. Validity is a measure of how reliable your research is. An investigation can be said to have validity if the researcher is aware of and has taken account of the variables that affect the investigation or the way the data collection methods may affect the population and sample.

For example in an investigation that looks at potential bias against Muslims in British newspapers, it would be possible to select only articles that carried negative bias. The analysis would then 'prove' the hypothesis, but the research would not be valid because the sample (the articles that are biased against Muslims) may not be representative of the population (all the articles about Muslims).

To give another example, if you were looking at the conversational skills of children in a multicultural environment and only looked at the skills of six-year-old Asian girls, your data would not be valid for other populations (e.g. six-year-old Asian boys).

Activity 22

You are planning to carry out an investigation into the conversation skills of seven-year-old girls. You have permission to select your subjects from a school in your area. Working in groups, base your answers to the following questions on a school you know.

1 How would you define the population for your investigation? Would you be able to define it as 'all the seven-year-old girls in the school' or are there other factors you would need to take into consideration?

2 What key characteristics do this group share? Do they have anything in common apart from being aged seven, being female and attending this specific school?

3 Which ones may vary across the population? (You could look at ethnicity, first language, social or cultural group.)

4 How would you take these factors into account when you identified your sample?

Activity 23

You are planning to carry out an investigation into the way newspapers report a specific major story.

1 Go into a newsagent's and look at the range of papers available. These might include national papers, regional papers, weekly papers, special interest papers (e.g. *The Financial Times* or the *Times Educational Supplement*).

   a Which newspapers report the same story as their lead story?

   b Which newspapers have the same stories on the front page?

2 If you are going to follow the way newspapers report a national or international story, which ones will be your population from which your subjects (a range of articles) will be drawn?

3 How would your decisions differ if the story was only of regional interest?

Remember not to make quick assumptions about your population. Some schools may be fairly uniform as to social and cultural group, others may be very diverse. You need to be aware of how this will affect your data. Similarly, different types of newspapers have different agendas, and you need to be aware of these.

An example of early research into language: William Labov's research on New York City speech

In the early 1960s, the study of language was in its very early stages. Very few, if any, linguists had attempted to study language 'in the wild' – language as people use it in everyday contexts. One of the first researchers – one of the first sociolinguists – to do this was William Labov. In 1966, he published a paper entitled 'The social stratification of English in New York City department stores'.

His work on New York City speech suggested to him that there were systematic differences in the use of language between different social groups. He also observed that a clear marker between those higher and lower on the social scale was the pronunciation of the phoneme /r/ following a vowel. This pronunciation is seen as having low prestige in the UK, but in America it is seen as a marker of high social status. He formed a hypothesis: If any two subgroups of New York City speakers are ranked in a scale of social stratification, then they will be ranked in the same order by their differential use of /r/. In other words, people's social group will match their pronunciation of this phoneme.

Activity 24

The extract overleaf explains some of the ways Labov decided to carry out his research into his hypothesis.

Working in groups, discuss Labov's hypothesis and the methods he is suggesting for carrying out this research. Try to answer the following questions:

a Is Labov's research descriptive, question based or hypothesis based?

b What are the populations and what are the samples?

c What variables can be applied to the research? Consider language variables and variables in the subjects.

d Does the research, in your view, have validity?

- Can you identify factors other than those Labov is observing that might affect the way people speak?
- Can Labov's findings be extended to apply to a larger or a different group?

It would be easy to test this hypothesis by comparing occupational groups, which are among the most important indexes of social stratification. We could, for example, take a group of lawyers, a group of file clerks, and a group of janitors. But this would hardly go beyond the indications of the exploratory interviews, and

5 such an extreme example of differentiation would not provide a very exacting test of the hypothesis. It should be possible to show that the hypothesis is so general, and the differential use of (r) pervades New York City so thoroughly, that fine social differences will be reflected in the index as well as gross ones.

It therefore seemed best to construct a very severe test by finding a subtle

10 case of stratification within a single occupational group: in this case, the sales people of large department stores in Manhattan. If we select three large department stores, from the top, middle, and bottom of the price and fashion scale, we can expect that the customers will be socially stratified. Would we expect the sales people to show a comparable stratification? Such a position

15 would depend upon two correlations: between the status ranking of the stores and the ranking of parallel jobs in the three stores; and between the jobs and the behavior of the persons who hold those jobs. These are not unreasonable assumptions. C. Wright Mills points out that salesgirls in large department stores tend to borrow prestige from their customers, or at least make an effort in that

20 direction. It appears that a person's own occupation is more closely correlated with his linguistic behavior—for those working actively—than any other single social characteristic. The evidence presented here indicates that the stores are objectively differentiated in a fixed order, and that jobs in these stores are evaluated by employees in that order. Since the product of social differentiation

25 and evaluation, no matter how minor, is social stratification of the employees in the three stores, the hypothesis will predict the following result: salespeople in the highest-ranked store will have the highest values of (r); those in the middle-ranked store will have intermediate values of (r); and those in the lowest-ranked store will show the lowest values. If this result holds true, the hypothesis will

30 have received confirmation in proportion to the severity of the test.

from '*The Social Stratification of (r) in New York City department stores*'.
Labov (1966)

Labov's researchers went into the department stores and, posing as customers needing directions, got as many sales people as possible to say the phrase 'Fourth floor' twice – once as a quick response and once, by pretending not to have heard the answer, to get a more careful pronunciation.

Activity 25

Below are extracts from the two student investigations described in Activity 21. You have already discussed the research parameters for these investigations. The extracts are from the methodology sections and discuss the issues involved in data collection.

1 Evaluate the data collection methods of each investigation.

 a Will the data allow the student to answer the research question?

 b What is the population? Who are the subjects?

 c What variables might affect the data and how has the student taken account of these?

 d Will the data be valid?

2 Now apply these questions and your evaluations to your own investigation and decide on your own data collection: the population, the subjects, the variables and the validity.

Student D:
Are gender differences in language identifiable at the age of 8?

My intention is to look at interaction and specifically at the language of negotiation and decision-making. A great deal of research into gender differences in language suggests that males are dominant speakers and that women will be less assertive when it comes to putting forward their points of view. I wanted to put the children into a position where they had to discuss, negotiate and decide, and see if I could identify any patterns that occurred that might be related to gender.

A potential problem was that some children are more confident and more dominant than others, and I might identify differences that were more to do with an individual child's personality or social and cultural background than his or her gender.

Data collection: stage 1

I therefore asked the teacher in charge of Year 5 in X school to identify the four most confident boys and the four most confident girls in the year group. I told the children that I was researching computer games and asked them to tell me which games they liked. I selected one that involved negotiation and decision-making and was popular with both groups. I then observed and recorded them playing the first stage of the game in single sex groups.

Data collection: stage 2

I identified from the recording the two from each group who were most dominant. I used several factors to judge this: taking their turns in the discussion, taking the lead in decision-making, supporting their own decisions or the decision they decided was the correct one successfully. I then put these four children together to play the next stage of the game. I video-recorded them while they did so.

Student E:
Can gender differences be identified in a group of 17-year-old speakers who know each other well?

I wanted to collect examples of the language my friends use in everyday situations, as I don't believe that the differences in speech styles that some researchers say come from gender do come from gender. I think it depends on the individual speaker, the situation when they are speaking, how confident they feel and who they are talking to.

I decided I wanted to collect a group conversation and analyse the differences between the way the boys and girls use language and then divide the group into male and female so I could record their conversation in single sex groups.

The first recording took place in an unused classroom. I was there to do the recording for each collection, but I didn't participate in the conversation. I asked them to have a conversation and I recorded this for 30 minutes. The second and third recordings took place at different times as I had to be there to record each one. The boys' conversation took place in an empty classroom and the girls' took place in a quiet corner of the common room.

Independent research

The complete paper is available in *Sociolinguistic Patterns* by William Labov. Read it and see if your answers to the questions in Activity 24 have changed. Can you think of a way similar research could be carried out in a UK city?

Coursework milestone

Check your diary. Are you on target with your current milestone? At this stage you should have identified your population and sample. You should also be aware of any issues that might affect the validity of your data.

Key term

• Observer's paradox

Collecting spoken language

The collection of spontaneous spoken language takes careful planning. If the data collection goes wrong, it is difficult and time-consuming to set up the collection a second time. You need to be aware of the ethical issues involved in data collection: permission and confidentiality. Technical issues are also important. Have you got the right equipment? Is it working? (Are you sure? Have you tested it?) Have you decided where you are going to record your data? All these issues are discussed below.

Ethical issues

You *must* have permission to record someone's spontaneous spoken language from the person themselves or from their parent of guardian and you must have this *before* you carry out your recording. You must explain how you intend using the data and who will see it.

This issue creates a problem for someone carrying out sociolinguistic research because of the **observer's paradox**, that the language the sociolinguist wants to observe is the language that a person uses when he or she is not being observed. In your collection of spoken language, you have to work out ways of overcoming this. When you are collecting spontaneous spoken language, you need to consider how the observer's paradox might affect your subjects and how you can counteract it.

Activity 26

Do the data collection methods in the student investigations in Activity 25 take sufficient account of the observer's paradox? Can you suggest ways they could be improved?

You *must* also make sure that your data remains confidential. Most researchers make their informants anonymous by changing their names or identifying them by numbers.

Technical issues

Make sure your recording equipment is suitable for the task and is in good working order. Select equipment with a good, sensitive microphone that can cope with background noise. Make sure the batteries are new (and always carry spares).

If you are recording a group of people, it might be worth considering a video recording if you aren't certain you will be able to identify all the individuals by voice. If this isn't possible, try to draw a diagram showing the location of each speaker in relation to the microphone.

It isn't always possible to have an ideal location for recording. If you are carrying out an interview, try to make sure your location is relaxing and free from background noise.

Types of data collection for spontaneous spoken language

There are four types: **random collection**, **controlled collection**, **interview** and **media sources**. When you are deciding which method to use, you need to keep in mind whether:

• it will collect the data you want to observe
• you can overcome the observer's paradox
• you will be able to set it up within your timescale

- you will be able to manipulate the context if necessary to collect the data you want
- you can collect specific language variables (e.g. pronunciations, words) if you need them
- you or your informants will find the context intimidating.

Random collection

This is when you record some spontaneous spoken language that you hear around you with no specific plan in mind.

Controlled collection

This is when you set up a specific situation (closely controlled) or take advantage of a specific situation (loosely controlled) and record the speakers. An example of a closely controlled situation is a group task carried out by members of your chosen sample, such as a discussion on a chosen topic, a problem-solving task or a game, especially when you put selected members of your sample group together. An example of a loosely controlled situation is children playing together in a specific location, family conversation at meal times or classroom interaction.

Your informants should be sufficiently involved in the situation to forget about the recorder. The method you choose to collect this language will allow you to observe the specific influence of:

- gender
- age
- social of cultural group
- social context or situation
- role or status.

You need to decide what kind of language you want to record to investigate your topic. If you want language where people negotiate, discuss and make decisions, you will need to control the situation closely. If you want language where people converse, move around different topics, code switch and use social forms, then you can use a loosely controlled situation.

Interview

This is when you carry out an interview with your informant/informants. It is an appropriate collection method when you want to identify very specific aspects of language. Labov designed a style of interview in which he asked his subjects to read word lists and reading passages, before he moved into what he called the 'freewheeling' part of the interview in which he guided the speaker through a series of questions that allowed them to talk in a less formal way. He tried to overcome the observer's paradox by using the 'danger of death' question in which he asked each subject: 'Have you even been in a situation when you thought you were going to die?' He believed that recounting such an episode would distract the subjects to the point when their language became as close to 'unobserved' as it was possible to obtain.

Key terms

- **random collection**
- **controlled collection**
- **interview**

Activity 27

1 Do you think the 'danger of death' question is an effective way of overcoming the observer's paradox? What do you do if your informant says 'No'?

2 Think of other questions that might distract someone from the fact that they were being recorded.

A successful interview needs a clear aim. You need to know what it is you want to collect and devise a series of questions that will encourage your informant to speak, and also generate the kind of language you want.

Activity 28

Below are two transcripts of young children talking. The first is the complete transcript of an interview with a four-year-old child. The interview took place in the corner of a classroom. Other classroom activities are going on during the interview.

The second transcript is from a longer recording of a three-year-old playing at home. The aim in both cases is to collect a sample of a child's spontaneous spoken language.

1 In groups, discuss the following questions.

    a Which recording has collected the best examples of a child's spontaneous spoken language?

    b Has the interview been sufficiently planned?

    c Is the environment ideal?

    d Is the interview successful? What has worked, and why? What has not worked, and why?

    e What would you change to make the interview more successful?

2 In the light of these examples, what do you consider to be the best way to collect spontaneous spoken language from a young child?

Transcript A: Interview

S: So (.) what is your name?

J: Jodie (.) what's your name?

S: I'm recording you for this alright (.) so why don't you move there for me (.) now (.)what's your name again?

5 J: Jodie.

S: Okay (.) so what is the stuff you're reading now?

J: I'm just learning how to read (.) so I don't know.

S: Do you read here in nursery (.) or does the teacher read to you?

J: Yeah (.) Miss Neville reads to me class [pointing at her teacher].

10 S: Yeah? (.) cos' that's what I did at nursery (0.3) but I didn't go here (.) I went to M… nursery.

J: Is that up there [points to the sky] cos my brother goes there.

S: Yeah?

J: And my brother [laughs] was expelled (.) awww.

15 S: Was he really bad then?

J: Yeah.

S: What did he do?

J: Dunno (.) but my mum got him another school (0.2) and he's really good now.

20 S: Yeah? (.) so what does (.) oh hang on (.) cos I'm not getting this about your reading (0.2) what reading do you do?

J: I don't do reading (.) cos I can't read yet (0.2) I said that.

S: Oh (.) alright (.) but does somebody do the reading with you?

25 J Yeah (.) me mum and she reads to me at night.

S: Awww (.) does she read a bedtime story yeah?

J: Yeah.

Transcript B: Beth ironing

Helen: Come on you gonna to do some more ironing.

Beth: Yes.

Helen: It's fine Mummy's (2) what's what's what's that what's the table?
       What did you say?

5 Beth: The ironing board

Helen: All right OK what you/

Beth: <??>

Helen: What you ironing?

Beth: Some clothes.

10 Helen: Whose is that?

Beth: Sammy's (.) tend (pretend) SAMMY'S.

Helen: Right.

Beth: It's tend Sammy's.

Helen: OK.

15 Beth: Ssst brrr ssst *[ironing noises]* You be a mum and me be...

Helen: OK. What are you doing with it there?

Beth: I just ah just … dis is pile on on on box. Dis dis is mine. Dese
       are wet.

Helen: Are they?

20 Beth: Yeah I got to iron er (.) er MUM.

Helen: Mm.

Beth: Er er dat dat black thing is mine (.) not yours.

Helen: Which black thing?

Use the key below to help understand the annotations, this will advise you on the pace and speed of speech.

Notation	Meaning
(.) (,) or (3)	brief pauses or a pause for a number of seconds
/	overlapping speech
…	unfinished utterance or interruption
SOME	capital letters indicate particular stress and volume

Media sources

The broadcasting media can be a useful source of spontaneous spoken language. If you plan to use a media source, you must be certain that the data you collect will be appropriate for your investigation. You will not be able to control the context or the informants, so there are a limited number of topics for which this data would be suitable. Remember not to confuse spontaneous spoken language with scripted language, and vice versa. A lot of apparently spontaneous language is, in fact, fully or lightly scripted.

Activity 29

1 In groups, discuss each of the four methods of data collection described on pages 133–135 and decide on the advantages and disadvantages of each one.

2 Which one will work best for your investigation?

Activity 30

The extract below is from the methodology section of student C's investigation into the functions of children's questions (see page 126 above).

1 What kinds of data collection has the student used?

2 What problems has she identified?

3 How has she tried to overcome them?

4 Do you think these methods will succeed?

5 Recording children had the advantage over recording adults, because the children were mostly unaware of the tape recorder. When they were aware, in recording 1, they did not alter their speech style, which adults would be likely to do because of self-consciousness. 10 In recording 1 the children were shown the tape recorder and told what it was for and were pleased that they were going to be recorded. Because they are unconscious of the preference of certain social styles, they neither altered their own speech nor became 15 minimal in their utterances. In fact, in a short time they had forgotten about the recording and carried on with their task, conversing freely.

The ages of children recorded were Beth 3:8, Jenny 3:6, and Katy, Lucy, Daniel, Harry and Michael all aged 20 around 6:6. These ages are significant because the younger children are pre-school, and therefore likely to be less experienced in using social styles, and the older children should have more developed styles necessary for communication in school.

The recordings are made in different situations, to 25 see if there are any differences. The situations chosen are recording 1 – in a classroom (formal), recording 2 – playing (informal) and recording 3 – having tea (informal but with children of mixed age).

One problem with recording children is that they are 30 unlikely to stay in one place for any length of time. To remedy this, the children in the classroom were assigned a task of drawing and writing, which required them to be stationary. In recording 3 the children had their tea set out before them and recording was done at 35 the table.

In recording 2, of Beth and Jenny playing, I followed them around with the tape recorder. I did not want to put restrictions of movement onto Beth as she was very shy and this might undermine her confidence and 40 prevent her from speaking.

When the data were collected, it needed to be carefully transcribed to allow detailed analysis to be made. Problems with this were that children, especially where there are more than two, tend to speak simultaneously, 45 making transcription difficult. To overcome this I made diagrams of the locations of the children. The recording of the children playing needed several diagrams as they moved around. I did a first rough transcription immediately after the recording. In recording 2, Beth 50 had a very soft voice, which did not record well. Some of her utterances were impossible to decipher.

Collecting written data

Investigations that focus on written language appear to present far fewer problems of data collection. The data is static, the process of collecting it won't influence it or make it change. However, the principles of data collection remain the same. You need to be aware of the population, the sample and the variables. Don't forget: garbage in, garbage out.

Questionnaires

This section will help you to decide if a questionnaire would be a useful data collection method for you. It will also help you to design one that will be suitable for your purposes.

Questionnaires can be used to collect certain kinds of information about people:

- knowledge – how well they understand something
- belief/attitude – what their views and opinions are
- behaviour – how they act
- attributes – who they are and what they have.

Written questionnaires can be very useful and effective. You can collect a lot of information from a large number of people, you can analyse the results easily, most people are familiar with questionnaires and you are less likely to bias the informant as there are no verbal or visual clues given by the researcher. If you are looking at attitudes to language, the spread (by age, region, social group, gender, etc.) of specific usages or opinions about specific aspects of language, then a questionnaire is worth considering.

However, there are some major disadvantages. Questionnaires will only collect certain kinds of data, you might get a low response rate from your subjects, you won't be able to get subjects to expand on the answers they give you and you will not be able to observe them, which may mean you lose information given by visual clues and tone of voice.

Activity 31

Look at the following list of topics areas and research questions. For which ones could the data be collected by questionnaire?

Topic area	Research question	Data collected by questionnaire?		
		All the data?	Part of the data?	None of the data?
Code switching	When does code switching occur in a multilingual family?			
Newspaper bias	Are newspapers biased against Muslims?			
Representations of speech	How does a writer use dialogue to create narrative?			
Regional dialect	Are the dialect forms used in a Yorkshire mining village by my grandparents' generation still used by young people today?			

A questionnaire is a useful research tool, but it needs designing carefully if it is to be successful in collecting the data you want. How do you plan to collect your replies? Are you going to administer the questionnaire yourself or are you going to deliver it to your sample to complete by themselves?

Planning the questions is one of the most important aspects of questionnaire design. There are three important aspects to consider:

- the questions to be asked
- the types of questions
- the order or sequence in which the questions are presented.

When deciding which questions to ask, you need to think about the aims of your research. What do you want to find out?

Below is an initial plan for student G's questionnaire for an investigation into attitudes to religious swear words. The student plans to look at the ways in which words and phrases such as 'bloody hell', which used to be seen as very offensive, are perceived today among different groups. The research question is: Are attitudes to certain swear words influenced by age, gender, social or cultural group?

Issue	What the question needs to do
What age and gender is the subject?	Target actual age or age range, and ask gender
What social or cultural group is the subject? Does the subject have religious affiliations?	Establish the ethnicity of the subject, the groups he or she affiliates with, including religious group
What things offend the subject? Which topics/concepts are likely to cause offence?	Identify areas the subject finds taboo. These can be racial, sexual, religious, other. Which areas are more taboo?
Does the subject use certain swear words him or herself?	Establish if he or she uses specific forms? In what context?
Is the subject offended by certain words? In what context?	Establish where he or she expects to hear/see it? What response does he or she have?

Setting out your aims like this allows you to formulate carefully worded questions that focus on the information you want to collect. Remember, if you omit a vital piece of information that you need to collect, you will have to start again from scratch.

Wording the question

When you write the questionnaire, make your questions simple and unambiguous, and avoid **leading questions** (e.g. Do you agree that swearing is offensive?). If your topic area may cause offence, as a questionnaire on swearing might, make sure that as far as possible you avoid using terms that will upset your subjects.

Closed questions versus open questions

Closed questions will elicit the responses 'yes', 'no', 'don't know', unless you offer a multiple choice of answers. **Open questions** (sometimes called **WH questions** because they use the words 'where', 'when', 'who', 'what', 'how') will elicit more detailed responses, but can be difficult to categorise and summarise when you are collating your final results.

Single versus multiple responses

If you are looking at several items in your questionnaire, for example, a list of words that you want your informants to comment on, don't assume that they will have the same response to each item. Make sure that they can give you multiple responses if necessary.

Key terms

- leading question
- closed question
- open question
- WH question

Activity 32

The question below comes from a questionnaire designed to test attitudes to a range of swear words relating to religion.

Try to answer the questions as a respondent to the questionnaire.

a What problems do you encounter?

b How could the question be improved?

c Rewrite the question so that it gathers the information the investigation needs.

> Would you use any of the following words: damn, hell, Jesus, Christ, Jesus Christ, God, bloody hell?
>
> | | yes | no |
> |---|---|---|
> | **a** With your parents | ☐ | ☐ |
> | **b** With your siblings | ☐ | ☐ |
> | **c** With your friends | ☐ | ☐ |
> | **d** With your acquaintances | ☐ | ☐ |
> | **e** None of the above | ☐ | ☐ |

When you are trying to get complex information via a questionnaire, you must make it clear whether you want a single or a multiple response to a question. The question above does not differentiate between the words or allow respondents to say 'yes' to one word and 'no' to another.

Ranked questions

Sometimes it is useful for the respondent to rank a set of options by numbering them in order. For example: Place the following list of seven words and phrases in order from the least offensive to the most offensive: damn, hell, Jesus, Christ, Jesus Christ, God, bloody hell.

Rated questions

You could ask subjects to rate aspects of your data, for example:

> Circle the number under the initials that applies: VO = very offensive, O = offensive, N = neutral, I = inoffensive, VI = very inoffensive.
>
> | | **VO** | **O** | **N** | **I** | **VI** |
> |---|---|---|---|---|---|
> | Damn | 1 | 2 | 3 | 4 | 5 |
> | Hell | 1 | 2 | 3 | 4 | 5 |
> | Jesus | 1 | 2 | 3 | 4 | 5 |
> | Christ | 1 | 2 | 3 | 4 | 5 |
> | Jesus Christ | 1 | 2 | 3 | 4 | 5 |
> | God | 1 | 2 | 3 | 4 | 5 |
> | Bloody hell | 1 | 2 | 3 | 4 | 5 |

If you are collecting data by questionnaire, *always* test your questionnaire before you use it. Run a **pilot survey** to check for any flaws in your questionnaire design.

Data collection is individual to each investigation. The data you have looked at in this section won't be identical to the data you have collected. The important thing to do is to follow the principles of data collection described and you will collect data that allows you to carry out your research and answer your research question.

Key terms

- ranked question
- rated question
- pilot survey

Coursework milestone

Check your diary. Are you on target with your current milestone?
At this stage you should have:

- decided what data you want to collect
- devised a collection method
- begun your data collection.

4 Analysing your data

What are you doing when you analyse data?

- preparing your data
- deciding on a method of analysis
- identifying patterns
- generating tentative explanations for the patterns and seeing if they are present or absent in other settings or situations
- working explanations into a theoretical model
- confirming or modifying the theoretical model
- drawing conclusions.

The analysis of your data begins *before* you have collected it. In deciding on a research question and selecting methods of data collection, you have already anticipated some of your possible research outcomes. Your literature search will have helped you to see what other researchers and theorists have said about your field.

Avoiding common pitfalls

This can lead to a researcher preselecting data to lead to the outcome he or she expects (see page 124 on circular hypotheses). If you are aware of this problem, you can be careful to avoid bias in your data collection and analysis. It can be frustrating to have a promising hypothesis destroyed by an inconvenient fact, but remember, research that disproves a hypothesis is just as useful as research that confirms it.

Preparing your data

Before you begin your analysis, you will need to prepare your data. Spoken data will need to be transcribed, questionnaires will need to be entered onto spreadsheets, written data will need to be sorted and classified. Remember – always keep a copy of your original, unaltered data.

The methods of analysis you choose will depend on the nature of your data, your research question and your hypothesis if you have one. Are you planning a close, in-depth analysis of a small amount of data or a more general analysis of a much larger data set?

Methods of analysis

The analysis of data can be divided into two kinds: **qualitative analysis** and **quantitative analysis**.

Qualitative analysis

Qualitative data cannot usually be reduced to numbers. Data that is suitable for qualitative analysis include transcribed interviews, data collected by observations of language in specific contexts, texts collected to observe specific aspects of language. The analysis is carried out to identify some form of explanation, understanding or interpretation of the language and contexts being investigated. Most investigations carried out into English language at A-level are qualitative studies.

> ## Key terms
>
> - qualitative analysis
> - quantitative analysis

Activity 33

Students B's topic (see page 107) looks at oral narrative to see if structural patterns and patterns of content can be identified. The student carried out the investigation by collecting narratives about supernatural or strange experiences told by long-term residents of South Yorkshire. Transcriptions A–H are some of the narratives she collected.

1 In groups, read the transcriptions and classify them into three groups, using any criteria you choose. You could classify them by story type (ghost story,

dream, vision, etc.), by the person who had the experience (the narrator, a friend of the narrator, someone else), by time of day when the event happened, or any other classification you feel happy with. Compare your classification with those of other groups.

2 What have you learned about the data during the classification process?

3 Write up your classification in draft form.

4 The student carrying out the investigation prepared her data by carrying out a series of classifications, which helped her to identify patterns in the data. A collection of over 100 narratives about supernatural or strange experiences were classifiable into a relatively small number of groups. Compare your classification with hers.

In order to simplify the identification of common language features, it was necessary to apply a system of classification that would hasten the familiarisation of the project material. The material was classified using four criteria:

The environment: where do the supernatural events take place? This was classified into three locations: the home, a (familiar) place outside the participant's home, a(n) (unfamiliar) place outside the participant's home.

The time of day: when do the events take place? There were three common time references: day, night, no time reference.

The role of the narrator: who witnesses the events? Not all stories were personal experiences. Many involved a participant who had personally recounted their experiences to the narrator (distancing +1) or the story had been passed through more than one person (distancing +2, +3, etc.).

The type of supernatural event: sighting/presence of a ghost; premonition through a dream/supernatural object; explicable phenomena; alien sightings; folk story/urban legend.

(Use the key on page 135 to help you to understand the annotations)

Transcription A

This is a story that one of my students told me last year about her grandmother (.) her grandmother had lost a very precious ring (.) it was precious because grandfather had given it to
5 her (.) and grandmother searched high and low in the house for this ring and she'd lost it literally for about 20 years and grandfather had died in that time (.) and then one night this grandmother had a dream and she dreamt this ring was down the
10 back of a wood partitioning (.) and she woke up and she mentioned it to her son and she described the partitioning and he said that's in the bathroom let's go up there and take the panel off (.) and do y'know when they took the panel off there was the
15 ring so she'd actually dreamt about the actual real place where the ring was.

Transcription B

I had this dream and I was in a car in the back of the car and there were two people that I knew in the front (.) we were driving up a hill and there were traffic lights on either side of the
hill (.) and on the left-hand corner there was a [5] pub (.) and it at the top of the hill there was a big roundabout with a carpark in the middle (.) okay right (.) and on about halfway round the roundabout there was a co-op a big big co-op (.) erm and then about a year ago just after I had [10] the dream (.) we were going up this hill and I was in the back of the car and my mum and dad were driving (,) we were on us way Chesterfield (.) and (.) Id never been before but I thought I recognised it (.) and then my dream came back [15] to me (.) and I said to my mum this is strange I had a dream where there were two traffic lights on either side and a pub (.) and there was a roundabout but in my dream there was a co-op [20] halfway round (.) and my mum said oh well that must be just a coincidence (.) and we got round the roundabout and there was a sign saying co-op but it had been sort of disguised from view before (.) and there you go. [25]

Transcription C

I remember some time back now oh I had a niece who was the eldest grand-daughter to my to my dad she was killed at er Blackpool er from the car at Blackpool (.) a tramcar
5 came along and killed her (.) she was only four and a half and er (.) the next morning when I woke they sent for me to go to the phone and er when I got there (.) a message from Blackpool which said er I'm sorry to
10 inform you that er (.) your Betty's been killed with a tramcar (.) I had to go back to my father y'know and I told my dad and he burst out into tears oh it upset everybody and he said I knew this had happened I said
15 why and he said because he said I was stood at the front door he said about roughly about half past twelve and I saw her in the middle of the road her ghost she was there (.) he said a premonition that something had
20 happened to her and it all came true next morning.

Transcription D

Well it were about half a year ago now (.) and most of my mates wanted to go on ouija board but there were a few of us that didn't want to go on it like 'cos we don't like things like that (.) so we went into garage 5
playing darts while others were on it (.) and after about half an hour we went in back into room like and they were still on it and they told us that they'd got God (.) on ouija board like and he were talking to 'em (.) but none of us believed 'em like so we just laughed 10
at 'em (.) and then all of a sudden cup started spinning round table like so we got quite scared then (.) so we decided to ask him a few questions if it were really God (.) so we asked him like who'd won darts match (.) and it were one of my mates Nidgy that 15
had won it and it spelt out his name (.) so we asked him how much he'd won at darts like how much money (.) and it spelt out the price how much he'd won (.) which were fifty pence (.) and then my mate asked him what he were gonna do once he'd left school (.) but it 20
told him he was gonna get an interview for a job and an he'd get this job and get a company car like (.) so he went for a job a few weeks after and he got it and he got a company car as well.

Transcription E

Right once when I was really little and I were in my cot asleep (,) my mother was asleep right and my dad had gone to work (.) an they lived at top of this block of flats (.) and my mother
5 woke up and she felt really strange (.) and she opened her eyes and she saw like these two men walking round the flat (.) and they were like in spacesuits (.) anyway she were really really scared so she shut her eyes and she
10 went back to sleep (.) and she told my dad when he got home but they didn't tell anybody else 'cos they thought they wouldn't believe 'em and (.) anyway my cousin and my uncle came to stop at the house and they saw (.)
15 the same thing but nobody had told them about it.

Transcription F

This is true this one (.) a man was found hanging in Greasborough Woods near the dam (.) and there were various newspaper reports that (.) I read at the time and I asked some of the students as well whether they'd heard about it and strangely enough although 5
none of them had read the newspaper article (.) they'd already heard stories in the village about the incident (.) one story was that the man was found hanging upside down (.) and that the magpies had pecked his eyes out (^) another story was that in order for the police to 10
identify him (.) they had to cut his hand off and the skin was so badly deteriorated (.) they had to peel a piece away to get a fingerprint (.) this seemed a bit far-fetched but the stories went on and the final story I heard about it was that one night (.) the bloke was 15
called Carrot-top (.) by the locals (.) one night after the hanging after he'd been discovered (.) the someone was returning home from the pub going past the Geasborough Dam (.) and they actually saw this man had a conversation with him and then walked on (.) not realising 20
that he was dead and told somebody else the next day and then that's how the story got about.

Transcription G

We were playing (.) we were young men an'
we'll say about 16 years of age (.) and there
was our Len and my other mates and we were
all playing together and in those days there
was no gaslight so you could see how dark
5 it was and er (.) we all used to play hide and
seek we were playing in old lanes and back
of old houses and and this this particular
evening it was it was a big moon like and
somebody said (.) there's a ghost up there
10 don't go up there and we had a look at this
ere ghost well I'm not going up so (.) two of
us said well we'll go and have a look and we
went right up to this gate and all at once a
white horse came trotting past us (.) and it
15 was this white horse (.) and it and was a true
story (.) we were all frightened and thought
it was a ghost.

Transcription H

When I was er working at Norwood Colliery there
was (.) er four men who were working along with me
but they didn't used to come on (.) until about half
past one in the morning (.) because they it was
5 what they call a continuous shift working (.) so
they used to take them off about half past one in
the morning and then they'd go home the others
so they were travelling home about two o'clock
(.) the chap they call Jack Hudson (.) he was
10 walking down _____ road and all at once
he set off (.) somebody said what you running for
Jack? and he still kept running and (.) what had
happened he thought somebody was running after
him (.) and it was the echo of his clogs that were
going and the faster he went the faster they
15 went (.) and that's definitely true and he ran all
the way (.) he ran three miles (.) this man (.) he
thought that someone was running after him and
it was the echo of his clogs.

An important aspect of data preparation is to become very familiar with your data so that you can spot patterns, anomalies and unexpected phenomena.

Quantitative analysis

Some investigations require a numerical analysis of the data. This is usually the kind of investigation that collects a large amount of raw data, for example, a questionnaire. To make sense of this data, it needs to be summarised in some way so that the reader has an idea of the typical values in the data and how these vary. To do this, researchers use **descriptive**, or **summary**, **statistics**: they describe or summarise the data, so that the reader can construct a mental picture of the data and the people, events or objects they relate to.

All quantitative studies will have some descriptive statistics, for example: sample size, maximum and minimum values, averages and measures of variation of the data about the average. The two main types of descriptive statistics encountered in research papers are **measures of central tendency** (averages) and **measures of dispersion**.

To give an example of the different pictures statistical analysis can give of the same data, look at the analysis of the marks achieved by one student across a range of eight subjects.

Key terms

- descriptive (summary) statistics

- measures of central tendency

- measures of dispersion

Subject	Mark (out of 100)
Art	20
English	70
French	70
General science	80
Geography	55
Maths	71
Religious studies	10
Spanish	16

Key terms

- mean average
- median average
- mode
- range
- standard deviation

Mean average

The **mean average** is calculated by adding together all the values, and then dividing them by the number of values you have. A simple mean (total of marks/number of marks) gives 392/8 = 49. How well does a mark of 49 represent this student's achievement?

As long as the data is symmetrically distributed (i.e. if, when you plot them on a frequency chart, you get a nice symmetrical shape) this is fine, but it can still be thrown right out by a few extreme values and, if the data is not symmetrical (i.e. skewed), it can be downright misleading.

Median average

The **median average**, on the other hand, really is the middle value. Fifty per cent of values are above it and 50 per cent below it. So when the data is not symmetrical, this is the form of average that gives a better idea of any general tendency in the data.

To calculate the median, put the data in numerical order. In decreasing numbers, these are: 80, 71, 70, 70, 55, 20, 16, 10. With a sample of eight marks, you need to calculate the mean average of the fourth and fifth values:

$$\frac{70 + 55}{2} = 62.5$$

Which result gives a better picture of this student's achievement, the mean average or the median average?

Mode

The **mode** is the most frequently occurring value in the set of data. For example, if a company had a single owner who paid himself £100,000 p.a. and 10 employees, who earned £10,000 each, the mean average earnings of people working in the company would be £90,000, which doesn't give a very helpful picture. The mode is the most frequently occurring value in a set of data. In this case, the mode would be £10,000.

Measures of dispersion

Dispersion measures the variability of the data and how far each element is from the central tendency (the average). These measurements can include the **range** – the difference between the highest and lowest data element. The range for the marks data above would be 80 – 10 = 70. This measure can be misleading as it will be distorted by extreme values that are not typical of the data. A more useful measure is the **standard deviation**, which is the average distance of each score from the mean.

Statistical and numerical analysis is only useful if you have enough data to count. There is no point in carrying out complex statistical calculations and producing complex charts for relatively simple numerical results. If there is not enough data, these results will not be valid.

Activity 34

1 Look at the analysis below of a conversation between two people. The student is looking at dominance and using the number of turns each speaker takes as one measure. He has counted them across one conversation and has got the results: speaker 1 – 18; speaker 2 – 16, as shown in the following pie chart.

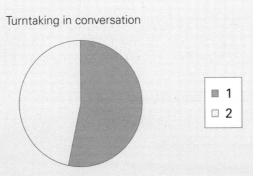

Turntaking in conversation

☐ 1
☐ 2

The second pie chart, from a different investigation, represents turntaking by four people across six conversations the student recorded. It was followed by pie charts for each of the individual conversations.

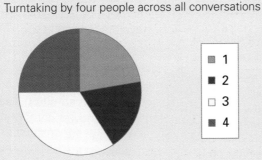

Turntaking by four people across all conversations

☐ 1
☐ 2
☐ 3
☐ 4

2 Which chart gives more useful information about who is likely to speak most in a conversation?

Language corpora

Corpus linguistics is a relatively recent development in linguistic analysis. Large bodies of texts (**corpora**) are now stored in machine-readable form and allow researchers to carry out a range of analyses that would not have been possible, or at least not simply, using non-electronic sources. They are particularly useful when it comes to studying how language is used. Before this kind of analysis became possible, much linguistic theory about language use was based on intuition and guesswork. Corpora allow language use to be studied by analysing hundreds or even thousands of examples. Some corpora contain millions of words.

Some of the questions that can be answered using corpora are:

• What are the most common meanings of a particular word?

• Which words does a particular word most frequently collocate (or is used) with?

• Does the particular word have positive or negative connotations when used in particular kinds of texts?

• Does the particular word have particular associations with specific registers or dialects?

An accessible corpus that will allow you some limited free use is the British National Corpus (BNC): www.natcorp.ox.ac.uk. The British National Corpus is a 100-million word collection. including spoken and written sources. The written sources include, among other things, extracts from regional and national newspapers, specialist periodicals and journals for all ages and interests, academic books and popular fiction, published and unpublished letters and memoranda, school and university essays.

Key terms

• corpus linguistics

• corpora (corpus)

Activity 35

1 What does the word 'snap' mean? List all the meanings you can think of. Which do you think is the most commonly used?

2 Read the following list of examples taken at random from the British National Corpus.

   a List the different meanings for the word 'snap'.

   b Group the meanings as far as possible.

   c Which is the most common meaning in this selection?

   d How many word classes can you find?

1 A snap decision to turn has been the cause of many serious stalling and spinning accidents, often when, in fact, there was ample room for a landing ahead.

2 Step-up roundhouse kick (a) Use a snap punch to disguise your step-up.

3 If you go into a corner too fast the tyres will lose their adhesion, but in the AX it is safe to take your foot off the throttle and let the car snap itself back into line.

4 So far, the Ramsdens have sent out 30 winners this season and they are hoping that they can snap up a tasty hors-d'oeuvre before the Newmarket feast by saddling their first winner at Ascot this afternoon when they run Line Of Vision and Hunter Valley.

5 This time the thunder burst with a pistol-shot snap and with an equal suddenness, as if at last those swollen vessels had been punctured, the rain began to fall.

6 In Jane's case, she could not snap out of a lifetime of worry overnight.

7 Silvertone are seeking a court declaration that four members of the band and their manager Gareth Evans are bound to their contract, among unconfirmed rumours that Geffen are ready to move in to snap up the band for £2.2 million.

8 Snap and toggle lacing system designed for triathletes £49.99

9 I do hope Chesky manages to reissue Wild's legendary RCA recording of the Scharwenka First Piano Concerto, but in the meantime all connoisseurs of superb piano playing should snap up this disc without delay.

10 Snap happy

11 That's why the hours spent achieving that snap on every instrument were definitely worth it.

12 A mini-buying stampede pushed the leading FTSE 100 Index to 2741.8, a jump of 32.2 points as investors piled into the market to snap up bargains.

13 Original features include narrow epaulettes, snap front pockets, collar snaps, leather hanging loop, hook and eye neck closure and underarm eyelets for ventilation.

14 Pap snap

15 His former manager Jimmy Lumsden admitted that only Dziekanowski's reputation for the high life enabled City to snap up the ball-playing genius from Celtic for a bargain £250,000.

16 Seeing the car as its territory, the dog may attempt to snap fiercely at them.

17 The squabbling became more bitter, and the adults began to snap at the children.

18 When too many snap, the whole web collapses into a sticky mess.

19 The door closed and then Elaine pulled the magazine in, from inside, causing the letter box to snap shut smartly.

20 Snap, Portia said.

21 The slightest kink in a wire and it would snap like a violin string, plummeting the flyer to the stage.

22 At last she stepped over it and went down, half thinking it might snap off her leg in passing.

23 Something in the back of her mind was saying: shock, you're in shock, Bernice snap out of it, woman, but she tuned it out and just stared at Ace until the world came back into focus around her and she heard Bishop saying calmly:

24 A cold snap, lasting at least a week …

25 You're asking me for a snap judgement, Miss Levington?

26 And it was several minutes before her quick ears picked up, from somewhere well ahead of her, the snap of a broken branch under a trampling foot.

27 According to press reports on Dec. 15 the Most Rev. Manasses Kuria, the Archbishop of Kenya and Bishop of Nairobi, who was head of the Church of the Province of Kenya, warned KANU against calling a snap election aimed at taking advantage of the opposition.

28 I remembered the larder was bare and took a snap decision to hit the local late-night deli.

29 This new date is selling fast, so if you want to see two fine comedians in one evening, snap up the chance as soon as you can.

30 In such a situation it is possible for the parent's self control to snap and in a moment of aberration he may strike the child in a manner that is instantly regretted and most unlikely ever to be repeated.

31 Snap happy … left to right, George Fletcher; George Cowley, Royal Liver, vice chairman; John Griffith, Echo editor; Tommy Howard; Michael Burgess; Stephen Shakeshaft, Echo picture editor; Rhys Long (front).

Activity 36

The list below contains 15 examples from the list in activity 35, showing the collocations of the word 'snap' (the words it tends to appear with or group with).

1 List the word immediately to the left of 'snap'. How many are repeated?

2 List the word immediately to the right? How many are repeated?

1 A	**snap**	decision to turn has been the cause
2 hoping that they can	**snap**	up a tasty hors-d'oeuvre before the
3 she could not	**snap**	out of a lifetime of worry overnight
4 ready to move in to	**snap**	up the band for £2.2 million
5 A cold	**snap,**	lasting at least a week
6 piano playing should	**snap**	up this disc without delay
7 piled into the market to	**snap**	up bargains
8 enabled City to	**snap**	up the ball-playing genius from Celtic
9 the dog may attempt to	**snap**	fiercely at them
10 and the adults began to	**snap**	at the children
11 When too many	**snap**	the whole web collapses into a sticky
12 causing the letter box to	**snap**	shut smartly
13 You're asking me for a	**snap**	judgement, Miss Levington?
14 in one evening,	**snap**	up the chance as soon as you can.
15 Parent's self-control to	**snap**	and in a moment of aberration he may

3 From your analysis, how many meanings can you identify for this word?

4 Which words does it tend to be used (collocate) with?

5 Is this sample big enough to draw any conclusion?

Independent research

'Snap' is used as a noun in the phrase 'cold snap'. Using the British National Corpus, search for other phrases to see if 'snap', meaning a period of weather, is used with any other adjectives such as 'warm', 'chilly', 'rainy'. (Use the format 'word_ snap' to search). How many examples of 'cold snap' can you find? What does this search tell you about this meaning of the word?

Other ways you can use corpora are to test the grammatical associations of words and phrases, their **discourse characteristics** (how they are used across clause boundaries), patterns in language acquisition, patterns in historical and stylistic change, and word frequencies. What are the most frequently used words in the English language? In spoken language? In written language? Analysis of language corpora has come up with an answer to a question that it was not possible to tackle before.

Whatever method you use for analysing your data, you should find at the end of the process that you have a more detailed understanding of the way the language you are studying works, you should be aware of underlying patterns that were not clear when you embarked on the analysis and, in most cases, you will be aware of further language issues that have arisen from the work you have carried out. These should be taken forward to your conclusion.

Explaining patterns

When you identify patterns in your data, how can you decide on their significance? If you are studying written or spoken text, patterns may indicate structures in discourse (i.e. how the whole text is put together) or they may suggest that data that looks very different is actually more similar than it seems. For example, researchers into Indo-European folk stories found a series of patterns across a very wide range of stories. The number 3 kept appearing: three brothers, three wishes, three quests – events are repeated three times before there is a resolution.

Independent research

You can explore some of the patterns found in folk stories by looking up the Motif Index of Folk Literature developed by Antti Aarne at Stith Thompson or the analysis of Russian fairy tales carried out by Vladimir Propp in his book *Morphology of the Folktale*.

Patterns may indicate an unexpected usage. In the corpus analysis of 'snap' above, did the most frequent meanings you found in the corpus match the ones you expected? Did they match the order of frequency given in the dictionary?

In Student B's investigation into oral narratives about supernatural experiences, she was able to identify the structures of oral narrative that Labov identified in his research into New York City speech. She also found that across 100 different narratives some other very clear patterns emerged. For example, there were only five categories of supernatural event in the narratives: premonition through a dream/supernatural object, alien sighting, ghost sighting, explicable phenomena ('I thought it was a ghost but …'), folklore or urban legend. The identification of these patterns supported her hypothesis: *If* oral narratives follow a pattern, *then* this pattern will be identifiable in a range of oral narratives told by speakers in a South Yorkshire pit village.

Activity 37

Students C's investigation into the functions of children's questions identified a range of patterns. One aspect she noted was that, in her data, the questions children directed at adults had a smaller range of functions than those directed at their peers.

Read the extract below and discuss these findings in groups.

a Do these findings suggest that children use questions differently from adults?

b From your own observations of children's language, can you suggest why these patterns may occur?

In the recorded situations, questions directed to adults were either straightforward clarification requests or requests for information or permission. When addressing peers, the **interrogative** was used for a greater variety of functions, for example:

- single word or short statement with a questioning intonation to express disbelief or challenge a previous utterance
- to make fun or to joke
- to build a relationship
- to satisfy their need to be successful in their roles
- to change conversational topic
- to make suggestions.